BLOOD BATH

IN
JASPER COUNTY, MISSISSIPPI

May God guide your

Steps

Walter Curiss

1/26/15

BLOOD BATH

IN
JASPER COUNTY, MISSISSIPPI

Based on a true story

MATTHEW CRUISE

cIIc

CIIC PUBLISHING COMPANY

Published by CIIC Publishing Company (USA)

ISBN: 978-0-615-41635-9

Printed in the United States of America

With Otis L Cavers

Cover Design Ron Odum

Historical Documents

PREFACE

My search is finally over, but my life is just beginning. I started searching for my ancestors because my brother James stirred my passion to not only find them but to return to our homeland. I have had the distinction of meeting people from all walks of life but I must say that my spiritual meeting with my ancestors continues to drive me to carry our family name with honor and pride. I have finally learned to love myself and overcome the disease of self hate.

As I began to understand the importance of family it has renewed my long lost desire to know the rest of our family. I recall my grandson Toyin Eric Dunn remark as a three year old I can't wait to have sex! I can't wait until the Census of 1940 is released in 2012 so I can locate the missing links that were born into my family in Jasper County, Mississippi and beyond.

I have climbed to the top of the mountain of emotion and continue to feel the very power of my ancestors; none more than my Great Grandfather James Cruise and my dear brother James Cruise. I pray that this book will spur others to locate their ancestors because a tree without roots will fall in the first wind storm.

I had the pleasure of participating as a speaker on a program for Juvenile teens on October 22, 2010; ninety percent of them had no idea who their grandfather was. I hope this book will convince our readers to make it a priority to locate their ancestors.

I am convinced that had I talked with my father and grandfather I would have healed those kind hurts that I carried most of my life. I thank God for helping me locate my ancestors.

DEDICATION

To my lovely Wife Barbara Jackson–Cruise

ACKNOWLEGMENT

I would like to acknowledge my editor Patricia A. Coleman who showed the patience of Job in teaching me the basics of writing, my agent Grace Ellis Adams who burned the candle on both ends to help me meet the deadline. She was a constant source of strength. Otis L. Cavers, my barber Bob Key, Ron Huggins and the rest of my golf group, Joe Warner, Emmit Hodge and Chuck Collins, all of whom encouraged me in the early stages of this book. A special thanks to Mr. Eugene Tullos of Smith County, Mississippi for his encouragement and exchange of information.

To my children, Matthew, Michael, Kevin, Evette, Marla, Randy Dunn and his wife Jeanette. The crew at Castle Print who helped me complete this project, and the staff at the Achieves in Jackson Mississippi.

To my Doctors who have brought me from the brink of death to a lively man of seventy seven years young:

Dr. Ravi Patel of The Comprehensive Blood and Cancer Center.
Dr. Augustine Munoz, Dr. Scott Ragland and the staff of Kern Facility Medical Group The Lab Staff at Memorial Hospital

My grandchildren, Toyin a senior at California State Dominguez Hills and Karynn Dunn a sophomore at Stanford University.

INTRODUCTION

Blood Bath In Jasper County, Mississippi will guide you through a vivid account of intimidation, fraud and murder, which had become known as common place, and for many… way to long.

The search for my ancestors started in 1945 when I was ten. My deep desire to acquaint myself with my ancestors was ignited by my brother James who at the time was only one year older. James would often talk about Africa and his desire to go there when we became adults. He would check out books about Africa from our small school library at Garrison School and would read with such passion you felt as though you were actually there.

James was considered wise beyond his years, even though he died at the age of eleven. In his short life he demonstrated wisdom and courage that belied his age. He helped shape my personality and character. There were many other amazing contributors who God allowed to cross my path. But it was James, who was my protector and my best friend. People that are still alive always speak about his intelligence and courage in glowing terms.

As our desire to learn more about our ancestors continued to grow we never asked our father or grandfather about their life in Mississippi. My grandfather Hiram Revels Cruise lived directly in back and one street over from us. He was a quiet man but we could never gather the courage to bring up the dreaded word "Mississippi." And he never volunteered to tell us about his life there. James and I vowed that someday we would ask him. After James died I stopped thinking about our ancestors. When my grandfather and father died within months of each other I realized that it was too late.

I grew up hearing bits and pieces about the trouble our family encountered when they lived in Mississippi. One day I overheard my Aunt Flora say "we had two uncles who were murdered in

Paulding, Mississippi." I had no idea where Paulding was and it was not until I reached the age of seventy three that I actually knew where it was located. It was at the same time that I learned the name of my great grandfather and the date that he died. We found his death certificate in the state archives in Jackson, Mississippi indicating that he died in Ellisville, Mississippi on November 24, 1912. His death certificate indicated that his father's name was Charlie Cruise, and his mother was Nellie Adams-Cruise.

This new information brought back thoughts of the haunting questions that lay just beneath the surface of my mind especially when some of the guys I met while serving in the Army would talk about their ancestors; I could hear the echo of the vow that James and I made to find our ancestors.

My cousin Vernetta McGlaston went to Mississippi a few years ago in 2006, to try to locate documents that would provide answers to some of the same lingering questions that James and I had shared years earlier. There are times when you think that you are the only person in your family who cares about things such as this only to discover that you are not alone.

Even though I had not seen Vernetta for over fifty years our desire to know about our heritage bonded us together...as close as a brother and sister. Although she is a great number of years younger than me she calls me baby like a mother would call to her child. I told everybody that I knew and those that I met and that I didn't know, about the new found history of my family. They listened with fascination and would always end up saying, "you should write a book." So after much prayer and meditation I decided to do so.

The most difficult part about taking on a project of this magnitude was to convince myself that there was a story that I had to tell.

When I began to consider writing this book I resisted because of my old nemesis, the fear of failure and rejection. The second was just as hard-deciding on a title. So far, the title of this book has changed three times and I am not sure if it won't change again. In my search for my ancestors I found a white school teacher, W.V. McKnight listed on the U.S. Census of 1860.

We learned through our research that he was a close friend of my great grandfather and had worked with him and many others to make things better for colored people in Jasper County. I have not been able to locate him in any Census after my original discovery in 1860. He and my great grandfather were instrumental in forming the Republican Party in Jasper County.

The answer could possibly be found in the Mississippi Historical Society Record of 1902, Volume IV. It seems as if he literally fell off the face of the earth. I have searched every available record and have not been able to locate him or his large family. Little did I learned that this young white man would play a significant role in the success of my family and many other families in Jasper County at the risk of losing his life…. and he may very well have. That is how I came up with the first title. "What Ever Happened to W.V. McKnight."

The second title came from the euphoria of locating my great grandfather James Cruise whom I had never met but yet spiritually was always my real inspiration for writing this book. He wanted us to know about his family and the extra ordinary things they accomplished under the in-human conditions called slavery.

He was a man who did extra ordinary things when slavery was at its peak. So the title then became, "Ordinary People Doing Extra Ordinary Things." I choose that title to highlight those who had accomplished great things throughout American History as it related to slavery in the South especially in Jasper County. It is my hope that those who read this story will be inspired to locate their ancestors and feel the joy of accomplishment as I have but most of all, to find some justice and closure, especially in those cases where lands were illegally taken from their ancestors.

After much thought I changed the title to "It Just Takes One Man" because in every generation, in every place, there is one man who in spite of impossible consequences dare to make a difference in his life and the lives of others. The ultimate man to and for me is Jesus Christ.

After a lot of meditation and prayer I realized that this was a much larger story. Not just a story about my family but a documented history illuminating a system utilized by white people to extract colored people from land that they rightfully owned.

In order to maintain my focus and clarity this story is mainly about two families who lived in Jasper County in the mid 1800's until many of them were murdered or simply run off their property. Similar acts happened to black families all over the South.

Some of these unlawful acts were initially reported by the Associated Press in 2002. Follow-up stories in 2004 and 2010 were published by the Jackson Advocate and African American Weekly, located in Jackson, Mississippi. The articles reported the saga of the Sye Lee family and his ancestors; and their desperate attempt to retrieve their land from "persons unknown."

After finding out about the number of deaths connected to the plot to unlawfully obtain ownership to lands owned by former slaves, it was apparent that a blood bath had taken place; thus I finally decided on the title, "Blood Bath In Jasper County, Mississippi."

Furthermore, a plethora of facts uncovering this diabolical system involving the unlawful transfer of land has been uncovered. This discovery is credited to the diligent research of James Edward Lee, the great-great grandson of Sye Lee.

James has been fighting an ongoing legal battle for over seventeen years to reclaim land owned by his family. His case is waiting to be heard by the United States Supreme Court. The Lee family's land is currently owned by Haley Barbour the former Governor of Mississippi and his family.

During discussions with descendants of former slaves, I was surprised to learn that in addition to the Lee and Cruise family there are countless others who have suffered the same fate. One family of note is the Pearl James Jetson of Houston, Texas.

To the average African American the word "Mississippi" brings thoughts of horror fear and human suffering. When I traveled to Mississippi for the first time in June of 2009, it was apparent that as soon as we passed the sign that announced that we were indeed in Mississippi that I began to experience a deep sense of uneasiness and anxiety, and yes some fear.

I was surprised by these feelings because I had served three tours in Vietnam and had been involved in a few fire fights but this was a different kind of fear. This type of fear unsettled your total being, causing feelings of uncertainty that the slightest wrong step or the wrong word spoken could possibly change my life forever.

It took Vernetta and my cousin Sheridan Cruise nine hours to drive from East Saint Louis, Illinois to the Mississippi state line. They did most of the driving because they didn't like my California driving style, which they said was a little too fast for their pace. The trip seemed short mainly because I slept most of the way. I woke up only to purchase gas and to see the sign that read Memphis...twenty five miles.

We arrived in Jackson, Mississippi around two o'clock on Sunday afternoon. After we checked into the hotel and I was settled in my room I couldn't help but think about the nights long ago driving through the south while serving my country I had to find a place that felt relatively safe because I had to sleep in my car because "negroes" could not stay in motels or hotels.

I was aware that I was in the place that I had heard about so long ago and none of it was good. However, I learned that as it is in all places, there are good people and bad people. I can honestly say that most if not all of the people that I met and talked with in Mississippi, were some of the nicest people I had ever met. They were helpful and friendly and seemed to feel a sense of disappointment when they could not help us.

This was emphasized when I went unannounced to the office of Mr. Eugene Tullos, an Attorney at Law. His office was in Smith County across the street from the historic court house. When I told his secretary the reason for my visit she went to his office and upon her return she told me that I would have to wait but he would see me as soon as he could. While seated I noticed that his walls were a pictorial history of the County that included both black and white families.

Mr. Tullos had helped write a book about Smith County which included some of his and my ancestors on the Ellis side of my family. About two hours later he still had one client. A mother waited with her son who had been involved in an accident. He had a full length cast on his left leg.

Mr. Tullos finally appeared and took me ahead of them. After exchanging courteous opening remarks Mr. Tullos pulled his book from his collection and gave it to his secretary to make copies of several pages relating to my family on the Ellis side. Many of those relatives still live in Jasper and Smith County to this day.

While we were waiting for the copies Mr. Tullos received a most interesting telephone call. I could only hear his side of the conversation but it was obviously from someone who needed legal representation. He listened carefully and said, "I can refer you to someone who is capable of handling your case. I am a lawyer who works for people who wear bib overalls, and brogan shoes." I knew that I had come to the right place.

He gave me information from his book about the history of Smith County which included information the Huey P. Long, past Governor of Louisiana, was born in Smith County. To my surprise Lennon Bridges Ellis, Sr., my great grandfather's former slave owner was also listed.

I confessed to him about my uneasiness while entering the state and promised him that I would mention the hospitality that I had experienced, and especially his contribution and encouragement to write this book. I have named him and others who have helped me along the way; they are the men and women that span the period from 1941 to the present.

We located a deed of trust prepared February 20, 1920, signed by my grandparents Hiram and Gertrude Cruise showing that they owned approximately one hundred and sixty acres of land in Paulding, Mississippi, land where oil is flowing to this day.

I have tried to be honest and true to every person who I have mentioned in this book. I hope to convince my readers that one man can make a difference in spite of the circumstances that life deals him. This book is about people who in many cases lost their lives in pursuit of the "American Dream" to own land, raise families and to become productive citizens.

From its conception the driving forces behind this effort to write this book are my cousins: Carl Brinkley a genealogist and retired police captain who resides in East St. Louis, Illinois, Vernetta McGlaston a retired school teacher who lives in Chicago, Illinois, and Sherri Mason Calhoun of Portland, Oregon, all of whom introduced me to the art and science of genealogy. I can't emphasize enough the impact of Vernetta's efforts that inspired me to write this book. Without all of them this project would have never happened.   To all of them, our family owes a debt of gratitude that we can never pay.

The setting for this book takes place in Jasper County, Mississippi. The place where my great grandfather lived from the time he was brought from The Blue Ridge Mountains in Picken County, Georgia to Jasper County, Mississippi when he was about twelve years old, and where he remained until his death on November 24 1912.   He was born in Georgia around 1834.   This is his story, narrated as he sat on his daughter Rosie's front porch, approximately one month prior to his death.

TABLE OF CONTENTS

CHAPTER 1
HOW IT ALL STARTED   21
James Cruise tells about his ancestors and when he was sold to a businessman from Paulding, Mississippi. He takes us through the early days in Pickin County, Georgia.

CHAPTER 2
FROM A BOY TO A MAN   25
James, tell about his continuing growth from a young slave to a man, and the development of a life-long relationship with his former slave owner. About how he learned to read and write while still a slave.

CHAPTER 3
LOVE AND FAMILY   35
Gives insights of life as a slave and how he met his wife-to-be and the life-long love affair that they shared during and after slavery was abolished. He continues to inform us about the developing dilemma that his slave master struggled with regarding the morality of owning slaves.

From Poverty (PUFP) and his trip back to Kenya, the place that he believes is his ancestors original home.

CHAPTER 1

HOW IT ALL STARTED

My name is James Cruise. I was born in the Blue Ridge Mountains of Georgia about1834, but for a very good part of my life I lived at what was called Beat 1, Jasper County, Mississippi, in the town of Paulding. This is my story, a story about my ancestors and my descendants. This is our story.

My father's name was Charlie Cruise, whose mother was born in Africa around 1790; he was born in the Blue Ridge Mountains of Georgia about 1810; the father of James Cruise, born in the Blue Ridge Mountains of Georgia about 1834, the father of Hiram Revels Cruise, born in Jasper County Mississippi January 3, 1877, the father of Frederick Douglas Cruise, born in Jasper County, Mississippi on July 11, 1905, the father of Matthew Cruise, born in East St. Louis Illinois on May 1, 1935, the father of Matthew Jonathan Cruise, born in East St. Louis, Illinois on November 10, 1957. These men are the direct descendants of a woman who was born in Africa about 1790.

The Chamber of Commerce of Paulding, Mississippi notes that it is located in eastern Mississippi, and was settled in 1833. It was named for John Paulding, a local Revolutionary War hero. He aided in the capture of the British Spy, Major Andre who conspired with Benedict Arnold in the betrayal of West Point, New York. Paulding was a thriving and important center prior to the Civil War, and was known as the "Queen City of The East."

It was once populated with over one thousand people prior to the start of the Civil War. It was a metropolis. Its main streets were flanked by stores, and its homes were white framed mansions, many of which, I helped build. Court day was a spectacle, with most other activities being suspended for the proceedings.

Reconstruction devastated Paulding; and the scars ran deep. When the states were called on to vote on the thirteenth amendment, the Paulding delegation held out staunchly against its ratification. Partly because of their firm stance, Mississippi did not ratify the constitutional amendment, freeing the slaves until 1995.

Soon after reconstruction, a railroad was to be built through Paulding. The county refused to help pay, even though the citizens could afford it. However, we heard the real reason for the railroad not being built was because the white women kept complaining about the smoke from the trains. Their complaint was that the smoke would dirty their white clothes. So Paulding was dealt with a death blow and the railroad was built in nearby Bay Springs instead.

From about 1866 to about 1910, life in Paulding was no better or worse for colored people; no matter what happened, we stuck together, and we survived. Life was well defined by white people. They continued to use the old system of slavery, and another form of it, what they called the Black Code. Peace among white and colored people was uneventful, because most colored people "stayed in their place."

I am now seventy eight years old, give or take a few years; it really don't matter. Because, as I sit here on my daughter Alice's front porch, in what is now called Ellisville, named after the same family that Mr. Lennon Ellis belonged to, I am trapped in my body, able to remember things a long time ago, but I can't remember when I got out of bed this morning.

I heard Doctor Carter tell my daughter that I am insane and senile, can't say that I understand it all, all I really know is, I don't get hungry much anymore. Still, I can remember all of the twists and turns that my life has taken, both as a slave, in Georgia and Mississippi, and the feeling of being a free man; as clearly as I remember the day that Mr. Ellis sold me the one hundred sixty acres of land in 1866.

Like the leaves that have fallen from the trees, as I look out to my daughter's front yard, with the back drop of the tall pine trees leaning on the hill side; they still hold on to their greenery in spite of the coming winter. I am slowly moving toward the end and yet my children and their children's children, like the evergreens nearby, will continue to sprout green leaves of life and happiness until the good Lord returns. But lest I tell my story now, it too will be lost and swallowed up by the earth, the same as the autumn leaves that are covering the ground.

My parents had six other children that I know about Charles, Peter, and Joseph; my beautiful sisters, Clara, Susan and Barbari. I named two of my sons after two of my brothers, and one daughter after my sister Barbari.

There has been a weight on my chest for most of my life. It is the feeling of being picked up and dropped into a deep dark well. It was the way I felt the day that I was separated from my family and sold to my new owner. I was sold the same way a white man would sell a mule or a cow. This said to me that I was less than human, with no heart, or soul. I felt that my spirit had been ripped right out of my chest.

I think that we should all know where and from whom we came from. That is the comfort that I get from telling my story. Those who will come along after I have gone to see my maker will know about our dreams, our fears, and yes our hopes. But not just for our family but for our country.

So, by telling the story of my family gives me great comfort and at the same time, great pain. Yet, a sense of completeness because I realize that the end of my life is near, and I will see them in the great beyond.

23

1910 United States Federal Census

Name:	**Joseph H Cruise**
Age in 1910:	36
Estimated Birth Year:	abt 1874
Birthplace:	Mississippi
Relation to Head of House:	Head
Father's Birth Place:	Mississippi
Mother's Birth Place:	Mississippi
Spouse's Name:	Beulah
Home in 1910:	Beat 1, Jasper, Mississippi
Marital Status:	Married
Race:	Mulatto
Gender:	Male
Neighbors:	View others on page

Household Members	Name	Age
	Joseph H Cruise	36
	Beulah Cruise	38
	Anna L Cruise	9
	Richard C Cruise	2

CHAPTER 2

FROM A BOY TO A MAN

In my eyes, my father was smarter than any man that I knew black or white. I would follow him around wherever he was working. It fascinated me to see him take one thing and make it into something else. My father had a reputation for being the best blacksmith in the county. He was a master at making digging tools. It was during those times that he would tell me about his mother who was born in Africa. As a young girl she was the most beautiful girl in her district. My father told me that his mother was captured by slave traders and taken to Zanzibar where she was sold to a white man named Cruise who brought her to America as a personal servant.

My father told me he could not remember his mother's African name, that she was always called Lizzie. She said the Georgia Mountains reminded her of her home land. In Swahili, they called these mountains and valleys "Bonde La Ufa" which means, be blessed as you work.

She was tied to a bulk head and was only released to be fed and to relieve herself in a bucket. The only time that she saw the daylight was to throw out her waste. When they arrived in Savannah, Georgia, she was about fourteen years old. It took them a month to arrive in what is now called Picken County, Georgia which was in the Blue Ridge Mountains.

My mother worked as a servant for Mr. Cruise's wife. I can't think of one thing that my father didn't know or couldn't figure out. We had to get up early in the morning to complete our chores and go to work. Mama went to the big house and my father and I went to the Smith Shop. Before going to the shop I had to draw the water for the day. I had to be careful because snakes would curl up at the base of the well especially in the summer time. If I

25

wasn't careful I could have gotten bit. It never took me more than ten minutes to take the water to my mother unless it was winter. Then I was also responsible for carrying wood to the big house as well.

Afterwards I would run to the barn where I would sit quietly and watch my father fix or make whatever tool that was needed on the farm. He also made tools for people as far away as Atlanta and Savannah. I was too small to work in the mines or be hired out. Although our master owned a lot of land he was mostly concerned with mining for marble. My father would talk out loud as he tried to solve problems. I could see and hear how he was thinking. The only food that Mr. Cruise grew was for his family, his slaves and the few animals that he owned.

It was common in those parts for slave owners to allow close slaves, slaves who receive orders directly from the owners, were often allowed to marry. Many of them worked in the master's house, or possessed useful skills. These and a few other slaves were more valuable to them, such as carpenters, blacksmiths and stone cutters.

Because most of them had white fathers they could easily pass themselves off as white. Their skin color made it easier for them to escape. The slave owner's believed if they allowed them to marry the slaves would consider themselves as Colored Christians and a family. In fact, most of them did not run away.

My father's master was the cousin of a Mr. Fitzsimmons. Both came from Ireland by way of Africa and England but they seemed to own the whole Georgia Mountains. I still feel now as I felt then, that it is wrong to take anyone's land, and just as wrong to remove people from their home land. In addition to his talent as a blacksmith my father quickly became the best stone and marble cutter and maker of fine statues in those mountains. He was so good that some of his work was sold in Savannah.

The Cherokees lived in those mountains since the 1600's before their land was taken by the United States. The few Cherokee Indians who were left after their land was taken were those who were sick, old or were expert marble cutters. The rest took part in the great march called "The Trail of Tears."

We were allowed to rest on Sunday. Because of this Sunday was always our special day to go to church, and be a family, and spend time together. Those were the times that I will never forget. I can still see my mother's smile and feel my father's hugs, and taste the special meals that my mother made. She would always surprise us with some new dish or a new way of preparing old ones. My favorite was fried salt pork, with fried sweet potatoes, and a cool glass of fresh cow's milk. As I said Sunday has always been my favorite day. But let me finish telling you about my father. He was the son born of a white man named Cruise and a slave woman. He was labeled as a mulatto but not a freedman according to the law.

We knew that Mr. Cruise could do whatever he wanted to do with or to us. Although my father was a slave he had a way about himself. If you didn't know him, you would think that he was a white man because of his light complexion he could have easily passed for white, and his thinking ability resembled the thought patterns of a white man. He was the first colored man in those mountains that could disagree with his owner (his father). My father clearly understood his boundaries and would only disagree if it were related to work otherwise he would stay in his place.

In those mountains, unless a slave committed a grave act or their owner was desperate for money slave owners would very seldom sell or break up close slave members. I was the first of my parent's children that lived. Two other siblings died when they were just babies, they had six more children before I was eight years old.

The first terrible thing that I can remember after being on the face
of the earth was seeing a white man beat a slave to death with a
whip.

I have often thought about the last day that I lived with my family.
As I went to the big house with my mother, I noticed a wagon that
I had never seen before. When we arrived there was a stranger
sitting on the veranda. As I got closer I overheard him say that he
was from Mississippi and he was returning that day but had heard
that Mr. Cruise had a young boy for sale who had watched his
father work with marble and steel. Mr. Cruise went on to say, "he
hated to lose the boy but needed money to purchase new
equipment." I thought to myself they are talking about me. I knew
that I couldn't run nor could I go to my father because I feared that
he might get in trouble or be killed if he tried to stop the sale. I was
sold by my grandfather.

About an hour later with no goodbye to my father I watched the
tearful stare of disbelief on my mother's face as I was put on a
wagon for our long trip to Mississippi. As we turned the bend of
the road, I saw my brother crying, I never saw my father or mother
again. It was the day that I met Mr. Lennon B. Ellis. When I was
thirteen Mr. Ellis secretly started to teach me letters. He told me
that if I learned to read it would help him when there was a job to
be done, and that I could study at night in my cabin. He sternly
warned me that I should never let anyone know if I learned to read.
Back in those days it was unlawful to teach slaves to read and if
anyone had found out, Mr. Ellis and I would have both suffered
severe consequences. I later learned to write and count numbers.

I practiced hard learning to say the few words that I knew. I later
learned this was call pronunciation and diction. It meant a lot to
me to reach this level of understanding. I don't know why exactly
but I have always been driven to know the meaning of words and
how to pronounce them correctly. Whenever I was in the presence
of white people I would often say the words in my mind correctly,

but would speak them as they expected me to say them. I took great pride in this little feat.

I longed to have my own book to read but I knew that if I was caught with a book there would be trouble, and anyway I couldn't read that well. Mr. Ellis had allowed me to build a one room log cabin near the place where the wood line began. Up until that time I slept in the barn. Mr. Ellis told me that my log cabin was built better than his house which made me feel very proud. Except for the day that I completed it he never came inside. Although I was still a slave it was the first day that I felt free, owning my very own little log cabin in spite of the fact that it was on another person's land.

When I was about fourteen years old I noticed that my master was not like most slave owners. He never spoke harshly to me and he was never mean spirited; but we slaves knew who was in control. I did not have to work on Sunday because he took us to church. He owned four slaves and we would walk about a mile to the church. It is the place where I first heard someone read the Bible.

I kept count of the number of houses that I build during my period of slavery. Since I could not write things down I dug up and planted a little flower bed for Mrs. Martha; when we would finish a house I would add a stone around the edges to keep count of the houses and stores that we built. The first thing that I did after President Lincoln freed the slaves was to run and count the rocks. To my surprise there were forty seven rocks around that flower bed.

We were set free about the same time we completed the new court house in Paulding. It was the first time I saw a Yankee soldier. Some years later, I took a trip to Savannah where I had heard that Mr. Cruise, my grandfather, had moved and opened a store selling marble slabs, statues and other notions but I could not find him or my family. Disappointedly I gave up and returned home. It was the last time I tried to locate my family.

29

Hannah and I wanted our sons to attend and obtain their college education. I heard that there was a school for colored boys. I had never seen anything like New Orleans before and pray I would never see it again. I guess my fear came from the fact that I had been a slave. And, although my sons were only one generation from slavery, they had never experienced the horrible things that I had.

There was a dance called "shaking a leg" was all they seemed to enjoy. White men with black women and in a few cases the other way around, they would walk down the streets in broad daylight and could be seen dancing in the many dance halls that was on every street. I have never been so scared in my whole life. I kept remembering the face of the slave who I saw killed when I was a young child. I departed on a boat the very next day. On my return trip I thought back about the time I started to feel like a man. It was a cool evening when Mr. Ellis knocked on my door. I had heard him coming so I opened the door right away. He told me that he wanted to talk with me as if he was asking for permission. He saw that I was afraid and said "James, how old are you?"

There was a sound in his voice that I had never heard before. I told him that I thought I was about thirteen years old. He pulled out a piece of paper that he had received on the day that I was purchased. The document stated that I was born about 1834, and according to calculations I would be about fifteen years old. I figured out later that it was about 1849 when we had that talk. Mr. Ellis motioned for me to sit down in one of the two chairs that I had made and he sat in the other. He asked me if I missed my family and without knowing what was about to happen I began to cry like a baby. For the first time in my life I was touched by a white man who was not trying to belittle, or harm me.
To this day when things seem like they are going wrong and I need comfort I can still feel my father's hug, the touch of Mr. Ellis's hand, the sound of his voice, and his look of concern as he tried to comfort me. He went on to say that he was pleased with the way

that I behaved around white folks and how I had learned to become such a good carpenter in such a short time. After much thought he lowered his voice as if someone might over hear, Mr. Ellis said "he wanted to pay me whenever we did a carpenter's job." He also warned me not to tell anyone about our arrangement.

You know that even after so many years I feel a bit uneasy when I talk about this part of my life. The part that Mr. Ellis played and why he was so considerate of me. I still have mixed emotions. After all he was still a slave owner and there is no denying that. It wasn't until he died that I could honestly admit to myself that he was also my friend. He quickly stood up and said James, he had never called me James in public or even when we were alone, tomorrow we have work to do and left without saying another word.

I did not notice until the next day when the sun rose that he had left a Bible under the chair where he was sitting. I was again gripped with fear because slaves could not own books, even if it was the Bible. As we rode to town the next day to start building a new jail my fear only heightened because I could not sort out what had happened within the last twenty four hours. I was not used to being treated like a man and now that I think about it, I didn't know how it felt to be treated as a man.

We worked as usual. He would lay out the detail and I did the work. We both knew that he did not have to lay out the job. He was always present but I never felt bossed. The only reason he was there was to make sure that I would not be mistreated by white men. There was some share cropping white people who thought that building houses was a white man's job. It was a small building and not too high from the ground so the work could have easily been done by one man. Whenever we needed help on bigger jobs Mr. Ellis would get some "hire out" slaves who were there only to lift and tote. The following week is hard to describe. Inside I felt fearful as well as happiness, and to this day feelings that I still

31

can't describe. Somehow I had to figure out how I was going to go about handling these life changing events. They had come so suddenly and without warning. I didn't know if I was in a dream or was I losing my mind or had God selected me out of all the other slaves in Jasper, County to help lead his people in a special way.

No one had to tell me and I did not have to remind myself that I was still a slave. My secret could cost me my life. Yet I couldn't wait to open my Bible. At first I would wait until the sun was setting but there would still be some light. I had a special hiding place for my Bible. I was anxious and nervous, I would look around three or four times to make sure that no one was watching.

I would go to my secret hiding place which was under two floor boards in my cabin. I hated dirt floors, so after I cut boards from a large oak tree that had been struck by lightning that spring. I laid a floor in the cabin. I would sit and opened my Bible, making sure that no one saw me. I never sat too close to the one window that was in the cabin. Even though I couldn't read at the time I felt as though I was looking at something powerful; just looking at the pages made me feel powerful. I would just stare and stare long after the sun had gone down. I wished I had had a candle but slaves could not own them. I was always careful because I didn't want anyone to find me with my Bible. But, sometimes I would fall asleep holding my Bible in my hands.

I would always awake before the cock crowed to hide my Bible. My mind was also full of the things that Mr. Ellis and I had talked about. What did he mean by "paying me?" Just as this thought was about to overtake my mind he came to see me. At first he just sat; not saying anything as if he was not breathing. Finally, he said "It's going to take us about another week before we finish the jail, and the Sunday after that I will give you two dollars." He changed the subject before I could think about what that all meant. Mr. Ellis said "I have been reading the Bible and I am not sure if owning slaves is right."

I just froze up and thought has he changed his mind? Just as fear was again coming over me he said again, "I am not sure if owning slaves is right." I felt as if all of the air had gone out of my body. I wondered if he could see the sweat on my brow but he just continued to talk. Mr. Ellis warned me by saying "before I do this I want you to understand that you should find a place where you can hide your money and don't tell anybody where it is located, including me."

I was filled with a joy that I had never felt, and still can't describe that feeling of joy that swelled up in me. He went on to say "trouble was going to come to the South about the business of owning slaves and the system of slavery might come to an end." He then said that he wanted to make sure that I would be taken care of if I was ever freed. I didn't know what he meant and just said yes sir.

The following Sunday I met W.V. McKnight, a white man; he was young, but older than me. He had come to teach me to read and wanted to know if I was interested in learning to read, write and learn the numbers. Once again fear gripped me but I realized that Mr. Ellis would not do anything to cause me any harm. I said yes sir. I think I had the biggest smile on my face if one could imagine such a thing. It was the happiest I had ever been. Just to think that I had a chance to actually learn how to read.

As Mr. McKnight was leaving I felt so excited that I was going to learn how to read I didn't notice Mr. Ellis handing me a candle and some match flints. He said you will need these to read your Bible. They shook hands and left me standing in the door of my cabin. Slaves were not allowed to have flints because white folks thought that slaves would burn their houses and escape to the North.

I sat dazed because I knew the risk they were taking and the trust they had in me. There I was with four things that a slave was not allowed to do, read, own a book, own a flint, and have some gold money. I was afraid to think of what would happen to me, Mr. Ellis and Mr. McKnight if anyone ever found out. We completed the job on the following Friday and true to his word Mr. Ellis gave me a two dollar gold piece. For the first time in my life I owned money. Money that I could not spend but it was mine just the same. I remembered what he said, that one day there was going to be trouble about the slave business. Until then I had never thought of owning slaves as a business.

I always cleaned up at the end of every day and would bring the left over wood home to make tables and boxes. Sometimes I would even make a chair. I began to trade chairs and tables for pies and cakes because I loved sweets. I made a small wooden box that I later lined with a scrap piece of thin metal. I heated my hammer until it was white hot and sealed the edges of metal together; a job that I watched my father complete while still in Georgia. I wrapped it on the outside to make sure that the dew would not soak into the box. I took extra care in covering the box so that my Bible would be protected during the rainy season.

For the next two years I was paid when we did a job. I continued to read the book that I had and by this time I was going to church with Mr. Ellis and his family on a regular basis. When the preacher would read or say a scripture I knew what he was talking about. Although sometimes the way he would say things did not sound the way that I heard it in my own mind. Maybe that was because I had never heard the words from my own lips. I was still afraid to read out loud for fear of someone other than Mr. Ellis or Mr. McKnight might hear me. I taught myself the sound of words and realized that words meant something. I understood why white people did not want their slaves to learn the art of reading.

CHAPTER 3

LOVE AND FAMILY

It was the last Sunday in June 1849 my life changed forever. I sat in the colored section of the church where we listened to services from the loft. During the summer months we endured extreme heat and even worst temperatures during the winter months. As I sat there I noticed the face of the most beautiful young woman I had ever seen. When I approached her after church service I could smell her soap. I looked into her eyes which seemed to sparkle like an early morning pond as the sun would dance across its surface.

I knew right then and there that someway and somehow, I would live the rest of my life with her. Her name was Hannah Reid. She was the maid for the Abney family. Hannah was purchased from one of their cousin's who lived in Alabama. Mr. Abney owned the bank in Paulding and was one of the leading citizens in the county. I couldn't tell you what the preacher had spoken about on that particular Sunday because my mind was not on the Bible teaching, but was on Hannah and Hannah only.

I had to be nudged by the fellow sitting next to me when church was over. It was common practice after church for families to "mill" around and share the latest gossip before going home to dinner. I just stood under a shade tree and stared at this beautiful woman. I was startled from my trance like state when Mr. Ellis called and told me it was time to leave.

He had a nice buckboard. You can call it a "Sunday Go To Meeting Wagon", pulled by the prettiest horses in Paulding. I would drive them to church otherwise I would have to walk behind the buckboard. Slaves were not allowed to ride along side his master unless the slave was driving. In fact, slaves were never allowed to ride on a mule because if he would pass a white man and he was walking, it would have been considered that the slave thought that he was above him, and of course that just wouldn't do. A white man would never stand for the thought of looking up to a slave in any way whatsoever. Mr. Ellis mentioned that he had noticed me looking at the new girl who was owned by Mr. Abney. He said that he could talk to Mr. Abney about visiting with the slave girl after church service. It was like I was on pins and needles the entire week. Just as we were about to leave for church I was told by Mr. Ellis that Mr. Abney had given permission for me to visit with Hannah. Mr. Abney warned that I should go no further than talking. It seemed as if my feet didn't touch the ground as I leaped into the driver's seat of the buckboard. It appeared to me that we arrived to the church before you could say the old nursery rhyme "Jack Sprat could eat no fat and his wife could eat no lean…"

Every time I saw Hannah Reid it was as if I had been struck by lightning. I had never felt that way before. So, when Mr. Ellis came by that evening, I told him about how I felt about Hannah. I asked him he would allow me to marry her? I told him that some Christian slave owners in Jasper County permitted their slaves to marry mostly because it pleased God. I remember an earlier conversation when he told me about the danger of slipping off into the woods to be with a woman. He told me it was about time that I picked a wife. I was glad that he was some years older than me because I could learn the most from him, about the least that I knew about…women.

I was relieved when he smiled. He was a tall man and in fact, both of us were taller than a six foot board. When he smiled little wrinkles would run around his eyes like the prints left by a leaf after the morning dew had dried on a rock. After church service, I met Miss. Hannah Reid face to face for the very first time. Although there were moments of awkwardness I could tell that she liked me just as much as I liked her. I knew that I wanted her to be my wife. So, right then and there I asked her to marry me. I knew we would need permission from Mr. Ellis as well as Mr. Abney.

Hannah told me that the first time that she saw me she knew in her heart that I would become her husband. I smiled so wide you could probably see every tooth in my mouth. I believed at that point I knew that there was a God in Heaven because He was the only one who could make someone as perfect as Hannah. I felt as if I was looking into the face of an angel.

 I will never be able to explain the anxiety I felt having to wait to marry this beautiful creature that God had given me. I prayed that God would intervene so that I could marry this lovely woman as soon as possible. Mr. Ellis took a job in Jones County that would take a month to complete. It was not the first time that he and I had worked away from Paulding, but this time I had someone on my mind.

We left early Monday morning because Mr. Ellis had to order bricks which were being made right outside of Paulding. My mind would go back and forth anticipating learning a new trade of masonry and Hannah. Up until that point I had only worked with wood and the only thing I ever thought about was being free.

Mr. Ellis and I had talked about many things and he told me that his wife was sick and he was worried that she was not getting any better. He questioned his decision about taking the job away from home. I told him that I knew a family that was part Indian by the name of Foggy who made herb medicine that might help her. I heard about them shortly after arriving in Mississippi. He told me how much he loved his wife and how bad he felt that he could not help her. We were about a mile outside of town when I asked if we could stop at the home of the Foggy's and get some medicine for his wife. Mr. Ellis looked at me with pleading and hopefulness in his eyes, but most of all trust. He just nodded his head and said "let's go see them."

Thirty minutes later just as the sun began to rise, as it only does in Mississippi, we pulled into a cleared area where three cabins sat. Richard Foggy was a tall man with brown skin and piercing eyes. He came out and asked if he could help us. I could tell that he was uneasy. I told him about Mr. Ellis's wife and asked if he could make up some medicine for her.

Mr. Foggy asked a few questions about her condition then he left for a few minutes during the time that he was gone we sat on the wagon and said nothing. I looked around at how beautiful the surroundings were. I could hear all types of birds singing. The air smelled fresh and clean. I could even smell the scent of flowers in what smelled like honey, and the aroma of pork rinds rolling from the cabin.

I knew that the Indian side of the Foggy family had lived in the area for years. They were run off their land because they had taken in some runaway slaves. Richard was the product of what the white people called an unholy union. He was the son of a white man from across the seas and a Cherokee woman. Just then Richard returned carrying a small bag containing bark. He told Mr. Ellis to have his wife chew a small piece of the bark.

He also told him to take a piece of the bark and break it up into three pieces and boil it in some water. After the tea cools, Mr. Ellis should give it to his wife to drink and have her go to bed. Richard explained that his wife would feel tired and sleepy but when she awoke, she would be feeling better. Mr. Ellis eyes lit up with hope as he took the bag from Richard and said thank you.

Again I could see the uneasiness on Richard's face because he had never heard a white man say thank you before. Mr. Ellis turned the wagon around and went straight home to give his wife the medicine. Without thinking, I followed him into the house and suddenly realized that although I had been there for over five years I had never been into his house except in the kitchen area to deliver wood for cooking. Mr. Ellis's wife was surprised by our return and appeared very weak and in some pain. After explaining the events of the morning to his wife Mr. Ellis gave her the bark to chew on and sent me to the well to draw fresh water.

I returned in less than ten minutes. Mr. Ellis's wife was already breathing better and sitting up in her chair. I can still remember the look of happiness in Mr. Ellis's eyes, for a brief moment I felt that we were equals because I was able to do something for him, and I knew that he appreciated it. The happiness I saw in his eyes was the same happiness I felt when I looked at Hannah.

We did not leave until the next day. About an hour into our trip he turned and looked at me in a different and strange way. It was as if he was looking through me and said "thank you," and I know he meant it.

As good a man as he was it was the first time that he or any other white man had ever said thank you to me. As I thought back, this was Mr. Ellis's second time. That evening as I was lying on the bed roll I couldn't help thinking about the things that happened over the last couple of days. Mostly, I thought about Hannah and realized that the hurt in my chest did not seem as heavy as it was the day I was separated from my family. I began to think and dream about a family, my family and how Hannah and I would be the best parents on planet earth. I knew that God was directing my life in ways that I did not and could never understand. The hole in my heart was replaced with a warm glow of expectation of what I had only imagined could ever happen to me; a slave boy without any family, finding a slave owner who treated me with respect and yes, was willing to allow me to develop a sense of being alright with myself, in spite of the circumstances that we slaves found ourselves in.

It was that day that I became a dreamer, not just for me but for all men and women who were unable to determine the course their life would take, deep down I knew that things would have to change; I just didn't know when or how it would happen.

U.S. World War II Army Enlistment Records, 1938-1946

Name:	**Otis Cruise**
Birth Year:	1920
Race:	Negro, citizen *(Black)*
Nativity State or Country:	Mississippi
State:	Illinois
County or City:	St Clair
Enlistment Date:	15 Aug 1940
Enlistment State:	Illinois
Enlistment City:	East St Louis
Branch:	Coast Artillery Corps
Branch Code:	Coast Artillery Corps or Army Mine Planter Service
Grade:	Private
Grade Code:	Private
Term of Enlistment:	Three year enlistment
Component:	Regular Army (including Officers, Nurses, Warrant Officers, and Enlisted Men)
Source:	Civil Life
Education:	Grammar school
Marital Status:	Single, without dependents
Height:	70
Weight:	151

40

CHAPTER 4

BUILDING A FOUNDATION

We completed the job in two and a half weeks. Mr. Ellis and I had other things on our minds. But, I took to the masonry work like a duck to water. We both wanted to get back home as soon as we could. Mr. Ellis to his wife, and I was aching to see Hannah. For the first time in my life I felt a longing for someone else other than my family.

I noticed that we began working more as a team, not a word was spoken, but I knew that this man and I had developed a special relationship in spite of the horrors of slavery. We arrived back into Paulding on Saturday afternoon. Mr. Ellis turned toward town and stopped at the Abney's house. He told me to stay in the wagon. It was alright to sit next to him when we were working because we usually had tools and materials in the bed of the wagon. Mr. Ellis returned after about thirty minutes, and as we pulled around the corner I saw Hannah standing on the side of the house smiling and waving.

Mr. Ellis smiled and said he would work out the details for Hannah and I to be married, but wanted me to be sure she was the woman I wanted to be my wife." I knew in my heart that I was ready to marry Hannah.

Mr. Ellis purchased Hannah a year later from Mr. Abney for four hundred dollars. He gave me the purchase ticket as a reminder of how far we had come. We got married under the tree near the church.

I continued to work building houses, and Hannah took care of Mrs. Ellis, who had gotten better, but still had times when it was hard for her to breathe. She always said how happy she was that Hannah was there to help her during those bad days. Most of those days had almost disappeared.

From the moment that we got married we began a lifelong partnership that lasted until she died in 1909. After her death; I would pass by the tree from time to time, and each time that I did, I would always feel the warm feelings of new love.

Mr. Ellis started to pay me a little more money soon after Hannah and I were married. The only secrets I have ever kept from Hannah were the business arrangement that Mr. Ellis made with me, and the business of the Loyal League. The day that I told her about the money was the day we became free. And it was only when she asked how in the world we would be able to purchase our own land.

My Sunday evening talks with Mr. Ellis continued. Instead of us talking in my cabin Mr. Ellis and I would meet in the new barn that we built between his house and the woods. It was far enough away Mrs. Ellis and Hannah could not hear us.

It was on this occasion, when he hit me with news that felt like a bolt of lightning. Mr. Ellis calmly asked if I had given any thought about the day when the government would free the slaves living in the South. I didn't know what to say, but I had heard there were already free colored men and women living in the North. I had dreamed about it but never really thought about it. Mr. Ellis smiled and said the strangest thing, James I know you are a smart man but explain to me how you can dream about something if you never thought about it. The way he said it caused both of us to start laughing. We made such a fuss that Mrs. Ellis called out to see if everything was alright. After we finally stopped laughing, Mr. Ellis became quiet again and said, "one day it will have to happen", and when it does he promised that he would do right by me and Hannah." I couldn't believe my ears, it seemed that I had stopped breathing I just said "yes sir." He sprang from his chair and left.

After that I learned to take time to think before I would give him or anyone else an answer. I developed the habit of asking anyone permission to think on a matter, especially if it might lead to danger for me or my wife. I wanted to be sure that any advice I gave was well thought out. It took me a week to give Mr. Ellis an answer but before I could, he asked if I would someday like to own my own land. He continued to ask questions that no white man would ever ask a slave. As far as I knew, no colored man had ever owned any land. But then again no slave had ever been paid for his labor.

This was almost too much for me and it made me feel light headed. I only knew that white men took land but this was way out of my level of reasoning that a slave would ever be free or ever own land. I kept all the things that we talked about in my head, and all I could come up with was this man, who by chance heard that a boy slave was for sale, was truly a good man. I was almost afraid to even think it but he was also my friend.

So, you might say we all made the best of a bad situation. Whenever we were alone he would talk to me about anything that was on his mind. I even began to start conversations with him…again something slaves never did.

A new lawyer, Mr. W.H. Hardy moved to Jasper County, and lived in Paulding for a period of time, and later moved to Smith County. Mr. Ellis asked me to get some bark and root medicine from the Indian man because the new neighbor's wife was sick and was experiencing some of the same type of symptoms Mrs. Ellis had experienced. Mr. Ellis wrote out a pass and a permit for me to drive the hayrick, which was used to haul hay from the fields. I needed the permit because slaves were not allowed to ride a horse or drive a wagon while traveling alone.

I waited until daylight to start out because night riders would still be out looking for runaway slaves. They searched for runaway slaves from the time the sun went down until it came up again. I wanted them to see me and see the pass and permit papers. I arrived at the house of Richard Foggy and the young men were busy getting ready for work. Slaves with half Indian blood lines were treated just as badly as black slaves, except they were allowed to live on part of the land that their ancestors had owned for centuries. I think it had something to do with their religion.

The white men thought they knew how to handle slaves, but were not so sure when it came to the Indians all of whom were by this time was a mixed race of people.

So, they separated them from the rest of the slaves. Most of them were "hired out slaves to companies that made bricks from the clay around these parts; while others worked at the mill where they used their hands to skin the bark from trees smooth on the outside, by scraping the wood with carefully selected stones. The wood was used to build fine cabinets in houses owned by white people. They had a knack for doing this type of work, and they did it better than anyone, whether colored or white.

On this particular day I got to meet the entire Foggy family. I got the medicine but before leaving I asked Richard if I could return to learn more about the art of making medicine. I wanted to be able to help my family and others, when and if they got sick. I got back to the farm just before noon. Upon my arrival I met Mr. W. H. Hardy for the first time. To my surprise, Mr. Ellis introduced me to him as if I was a white man. I was even more surprised when Mr. Hardy shook my hand, and little did I know that one day he too would help save my life.

CHAPTER 5

WAR AND CHANGE

By this time I suppose I was the only slave in Jasper County who could read and write. Nobody knew it except Mr. Ellis, Mr. McKnight and God. Thank God! Mr. Ellis was no longer helping in teaching me because he had become a leader in the church and in the community. On most Sunday's he would stay after church and go along with the other elders to visit the sick.

I would take Mrs. Ellis, Hannah and Mary, our first child home. Mrs. Ellis and Hannah had started to sew together. I am not sure who taught whom but they seem pretty at ease with each other. Not as a slave or a master, just two people sitting quietly on the veranda in Southeastern, Mississippi. I am sure it was because of the good feelings they had developed for each other. In another time, a passerby would have thought they were friends enjoying each other's company on a cool spring evening.

Mr. Ellis got a permit for me to drive back to the church. I would take Mary back to Church with me. Having my daughter with me brought back memories of the times that I spent with my father and the pride that I felt while watching him work in those mountains.

Taking Mary back to church with me allowed Mrs. Ellis and Hannah time to enjoy each other's company without the distraction of a little girl under their feet. Mary was about four years old and started talking before she was two she has not stopped talking to this day. I was tempted to teach her the alphabets, but I realized what problems that would cause. I knew that one day she would read much better than me but I was afraid that she would start reciting the letters in front of white people and that just would not do. I told her stories about my father and mother, and how I came to Mississippi. I loved my daughter so much but I longed to have a son. I had to wait another eleven years. In the meantime we had five more lovely daughters. All of them were the apples of my eye.

It seemed as if we were having babies every time the weather changed. All of them were girls. We had Mary, Caroline, Barbria, Ellen, Alice and Amanda. After slavery, we taught them to read as early as they were able to understand. When they began to go to school they were always the best students.

Hannah and I often joked about the fact that we had obeyed God when he said be fruitful and multiply and raise your children up in the nurture and admonition of the Lord. As we got older we passed the torch on to our daughters and sons who began to marry and have their own children.

I was glad that God made me wait for our son William Charles Cruise, born two years after Amanda. He was born in 1866, the first free man born into our family. Praise God! Most of the time, Mr. Ellis would have finished by the time we got back to church. However, on this particular day there were men at the church who were not members.

You could hear them from beneath the old oak tree which stood near the church. They were yelling and it sounded as if some were in favor of going to war and a few were not. In the middle of all of the yelling I could hear Mr. Ellis say, "I hear what you are saying." When the meeting was over he said a few words to Mr. Abney and we started for home. As we traveled, the only thing that Mr. Ellis said was "trouble is a brewing."

Times were changing in Jasper, County, and Mr. Ellis said the same things were happening all over the South. Mr. Hardy came by the plantation in the spring of 1859, and told Mr. Ellis that Mr. Heidelberg, a businessman who recently purchased some land about ten to twelve miles from Paulding wanted to build another town. Mr. Hardy had highly recommended Mr. Ellis for the job.

Our ability to build good solid houses played a big role in Mr. Heidelberg hiring him. It was the best job that we ever had.

It took us about three months to complete the first house because Mr. Heidelberg had purchased the best materials that the South had to offer. The brick work used below the large veranda, which framed the entire house showed his desire for detail as well as quality. It was the first time that a combination of wood and brick had been used to build a house in those parts. Mr. Ellis decided that it was time to see if the white people would allow me to build a house without the presence of a white man. It was against the law for a slave to supervise another slave, but it was one law that was often over looked, especially during the war. I heard the fine was five dollars if a person was caught.

Mr. Ellis asked Mr. Hardy to write up an agreement between him and Mr. Heidelberg. The agreement would allow me to work with two other men; one Indian and one colored. He assured Mr. Heidelberg that he would check on us every Tuesday, Thursday and Saturday, and if the houses were not built as agreed he would not have to pay any more than the cost of materials.

I don't know how they convinced Mr. Heidelberg to agree to the terms but I think it had something to do with him being German and not being accustomed to the ways of the South. With the exception of the occasional hauler coming from Amite or Paulding there was only the three of us. The few times we were asked about what we were doing and who we were by strangers, I would show them the permit to travel and the authority for us to work signed by the sheriff.

The half Indian that he hired was none other than Richard Foggy our medicine man. We never had any trouble. Now, Mr. Ellis was able to attend to some of his other business, which I was not involved in. Things were going well and we built a total of three houses and a one room school for Mr. Heidelberg's children. There were a total of five people living in the place that was later named after its founder, Mr. Heidelberg.

By this time his children were of the age when white children would attend school. Mr. Heidelberg hired Mr. W. V. McKnight my secret teacher, as their school master. Mr. McKnight had a habit of looking at me in a most unusual manner, not like most white people. Usually when a white person would look a slave directly into his eyes, the slave was expected to look down. Not only did white people want to control the body of slaves, they also wanted to control their very souls. Mr. McKnight tried to instill pride in me and he always tried to encourage me. We could always tell when a white man wanted to intimidate us, whip us or otherwise cause us trouble by the way he would stare at us.

Because of Mr. McKnight's consistent encouragement I would go to my secret hiding place and take out my Bible. I would practice sounding out the words that I had heard that day. I still was not able to speak the words out loud, for fear of being over heard, so I had to say them in my head. It was difficult trying to say the words the right way, but also remembering when in the presence of white people, I still had to talk like a slave.

I continued saying passages of scripture seven times a day, for seven days before I would move on to another set of scripture. I was able to remember every word that I had read. I later passed this method of learning on to my children.

I recall the second thing that I did when we were set free, was to take out my Bible and start to read it out loud. Hannah was so shocked that she almost gave birth to our seventh child. At first, she did not understand what she was hearing. She thought I was either out of my mind or I was playing some sort of game, which we often did when we were joking around with each other. When she heard some of the words that she heard the preacher say at church her eyes were filled with tears of fear but mine were filled with tears of joy.

I was like a man who had never heard a sound in his life, and now to experience the joy and mystery of the written word was another lifetime highlight. Even though Hannah could not read she knew what most of the words meant. I found my second love, the joy of reading. I was amazed at how words could take you places without you ever going there.

I remembered the time while building in Heidelberg we would stop for lunch about the time, school was over Mr. McKnight would stop by to observe our progress. He would comment on what a great job we were doing, and how he was amazed by my carpentry skills. Mr. McKnight would sometimes pull me aside and sing this strange song to me, creating lyrics by using the alphabets and this is how I learned how to sound out the alphabet.

 As I said W. V. McKnight was different. Although I continued to see him from time to time, I never thought our lives would later cross after the war ended. As I looked back over the bad times of slavery I am amazed at the power of God and how He used just one man to help save His people. I came to this conclusion after many years of reading the Bible. I learned that God always finds a man to lead his people to the promise land, and for us that was always the "Land of Lincoln"

In 1857, there were three lynchings that took place in Jasper, County just before the rumors began to spread about Mississippi not being governed by the government in Washington. The first lynching happened when a slave was accused of raping a white woman, and the other two were hung because they beat their masters to death. Everybody was riled up and said that unless they were left alone about owning slaves, the south was prepared to leave the union, and if necessary to fight for their right as a state. There was a lot of tension and unrest because most people in

Jasper, County both colored and white were afraid; colored people because we felt that the white slave owners would kill all of us if the Northern soldiers came, and the white people were afraid that they would lose their land and their slaves.

Hannah and I had four children we were all staying in one room. One day when I talking with Mr. Ellis; I told him that I still had all of the money that he had ever paid me and I wanted to add on to the cabin that I had lived in since he brought me to his plantation.

On the following Sunday after church when everybody had finished eating, he came and said that we needed to look at some land that he owned because he wanted to build a house on it. The land that he owned sat on top of a hill about a mile outside of Paulding. We had to leave the horses tied to a tree and walk up the hill. We found a flat area and decided on which direction the front of the house would face. The following week Mr. Ellis and I began to build the foundation.

He told the leading citizens about his plans to build a house and that he would start cutting down his timber in the area. Mr. Ellis informed them that he might decide to live in the house at a later date but in the meantime he would need to hire a man to supervise the slaves who would be cutting down the trees. We did not finish the house until August 1866, because the Civil War had begun.

At first things were the same for slaves but some white began to leave to fight for the right to own slaves, and do so without the fear of the government in Washington. Mr. Ellis began to sell a lot of timber to the railroads because rails were being laid in Southeastern Mississippi. I was the overseer on the main crew that cut timber on his land but he hired white men to take it to the loading area.

CHAPTER 6

THE CIVIL WAR

Most of the states in the South had left the union and formed a Confederate Union. There was a certainty felt by most that there was going to be some fighting. In April 1861, the Civil War began in South Carolina. It wasn't until June of that year when white men around these parts began to volunteer to fight in the war. It was a time when most white people felt that they had to fight to represent "the honor of the South." The war never reached Paulding. We never saw one Yankee Soldier until the war had ended. The only thing that we knew about the war was that it started and the day that it ended. The Northern Soldiers had won the war and we had gained our freedom.

About ten men from Paulding and the surrounding area went to fight in the war. One of them was Mr. Q. C. Heidelberg who returned home as a highly decorated soldier the other was W.T. Lambert. They both later worked with Sheriff Burkitt Lassiter before he moved to the town of Heidelberg; little did I know that our paths would also cross after the war.

There were few men left who could supervise slaves. Plantation owners in Jasper, County began to have colored men supervise colored men whether in the fields or where ever else they were needed. Mr. Lennon seemed to never take sides about the war but he had a way of making a person think that he was agreeing with them. He would always say, "I hear what you are saying," then the other person would think that he was saying I agree with you. Words do have meaning.

I knew how Mr. Lennon felt about slavery just by the way he treated me and the things that he had told me. He and I began to develop a plan to know what we would do if the soldiers from the

North ever came to Paulding. We knew where we would hide, and what we would say if we were caught by the soldiers. The soldiers did not show up until the Mississippi State Census was taken in 1866. We stopped building houses during the war and only did fix up carpentry work to help people because most of the people did not have very much money. Mr. Ellis began selling more timber to the railroad but things were hard, but then again, it was always hard if you were a slave.

CHAPTER 7

A NEW BEGINNING

During the war years we always had enough food and meat that was grown or raised on the farm. It was about August 1865, when Mr. Ellis came and told us that the war was over and President Lincoln had freed the slaves. I was stunned I couldn't believe or fully understand that I was actually free and what being free, actually felt like.

I was about thirty one years old when Mr. Ellis told me that we could go where we wanted, or could stay here and we could work out the details later. He reached out his hand and for the third time in my life, said thank you for everything and I told him right then and there that we were not leaving.

The next day as we drove toward Paulding he again turned up the road where we had began building the house before the war started. We tied the horses to the same pine tree and walked up the hill overlooking the town, the foundation was still there and the wood had cured.

He asked me if I remembered talking about adding to the cabin before the war started, I said that I did and he said, "I made up in his mind that very day that I would sell you a hundred sixty acres of land and would help you build a house." I understood what he said but I didn't understand what he meant; then slowly it became clear but I was still in wonderment.

We sat down on the ground in the red Mississippi clay and made an agreement that he would sell me the parcel for one dollar an acre and would give me ownership papers to prove that it was legally mine and it belonged to me. He went on to say "I believe you're the first colored man to own land in Jasper County." I said a prayer of thanks to God and vowed that I would never sell or leave. As we sat there it began to drizzle; I was glad because it hid the tears that we both shed on my hill top land. I knew that this was one of the highest points in the area, before you hit the giant woodlands. I smiled as I thought about riding a tall mule.

Hannah and I vowed that if God be willing we would die and be buried on our land, land that someday would be owned by our children and their children's children. It was with the same mind that we vowed to stay married

The world had been turned upside down but in a good way, a happy way. Everything that I had ever known was no longer true. Not only did I not belong to anyone but no one owned me. I owned land that I would build my house on, and I had money that I could now spend and could finally read out loud.

These were things that I had dared never dream of; dared never hoped for, dared never thought would be possible. I felt truly free and for the first time I knew for sure that I had been truly blessed by God.

I raced home to tell Hannah about our good news; it took ten minutes for me to stop laughing and crying at the same time. She knew that I had something to say something important; she looked at me hard and at first she was scared, but a look of joy came over her face when she realized what this all meant, we just held each other and cried.

As I look back on that day and the weeks that followed it was a high point of my life; however, I had a hollow feeling and something stirred in me that dark days were coming. About a year later Mr. Ellis moved his family to Jones County; Hannah and I had completed and furnished our house, and from the money that I had saved we were able to buy two cows, five pigs, a mule, and wagon from him.

We completed the move to our own land a week before Christmas! With our family that now included our first son, William Charles Cruise and our six daughters. We had enough room that our girls shared three rooms and William had his own room. What a change.

White people didn't know how to treat colored people, especially me, and we didn't know how to act when we were around them. We went about our business trying to build a new life for ourselves and our families while at the same time, staying clear of the white folks who had a reputation of being more than mean.

I no longer had to keep the promise that I made to Mr. Ellis about the money and the Bible and by this time, Hannah was the only other person who knew just where we stood, with money. When the Mississippi Census takers came in 1866, I told them that I was worth one hundred dollars, when in fact, I had almost one thousand dollars in cash, I did not realize how "well off" we were.

I continued to teach Hannah and Mary how to read and we became good students of the Bible. It was the only book that we had. In the fall of 1866, when William was less than six months old, the union soldiers came to Jasper County to oversee the count that was taking place in Mississippi; the census takers told them about us, and when they came to our place they were surprised that we really did own our land. They were equally stunned when they learned that we worked for ourselves, and could read and write.

They were so excited that the officer in charge, a tall good natured man, returned the next day and asked me how I was able to buy this land, and build this house. I said sir, it was by the grace of God; they almost fell out, when I told that that I was also a skilled carpenter, and had never worked in the fields. The soldiers also supervised the handing out of food and clothes to the former slaves, but the Freedman's agents took most of the goods for themselves, and would later sell them for a profit.

Since slaves could not read or write, the agents would hold their hand and make an X, for fifty pounds of bacon, and a hundred pounds of flour; but the agent would only give them half of the food. They sold the rest and made a big profit. I never went to the "hand out line" because we did not need food, clothing or shelter and I was not sure how I would react if they tried to cheat me, because I could read and would know what they were doing.

One of the last serious meetings that I had soon after Mr. Ellis moved to Ellisville, he told me about a group of white men who were calling themselves the Klan, and warned me to make sure that I gave no cause for them to ever bother me and my family. We later learned that they did not have to have a reason for them to try to intimidate us-our only sin was being black.

CHAPTER 8

THE LOYAL LEAGUE

All of a sudden colored people were holding offices at the county and state levels, and even in Washington D.C. in the person of Hiram Revels. I first met him in person at a Methodist Church meeting. Although I knew all about his efforts to help the colored people in Mississippi this was the first time I met him in person. I was so impressed with him and his efforts I named one of my sons after him.

I had never seen a colored man who was educated and could speak like an educated white man. Since I was considered a leading colored citizen he took note of me and he later played a great part in helping us to establish the Loyal League in Jasper County.

I was surprise to see W. V. McKnight, Mr. Ellis, and Mr. Hardy on the last day of the three day meeting. Mr. Revels closed out the meeting with a speech about the need for white and colored people to live in peace and that all people should be given a chance to get a good education or learn a trade. He spoke about the need for colored and white churches to play a major role in helping former slaves in their pursuit and their fight to own and keep their land.

I was not surprised when Mr. Ellis stopped by after church the following Sunday. It seemed that he was quite moved by Mr. Revel's speech. I knew that he would want to discuss it later and I was anxious to hear what he thought.

By this time the colored people had their own church and we could not talk after service was over as we use to do. I was living on my land and he was in Ellisville; therefore the only time we would see each other was to talk about jobs and the timber business but it seemed that we rarely talked business anymore.

He visited me on a Saturday morning the sun had just tipped its hat to the tall pine trees to the West of my house. He told me that most of the colored people in the county respected me. We talked about how things had changed for everybody and he said "I was one of real leaders at least for colored folks. I was one of the first land owners and it was commonly known that I could read and write."

All things any man would be proud to have accomplished colored or white. He told me how many people looked up to me and trusted me. He went on to say that he had talked with W. V. McKnight and they agreed that change was going to come. He said that I should talk with W.V. about ways we could help the colored people of Jasper County.

The next Saturday W. V. saw me in Paulding and said that he would like to come by and discuss some important business with me, when he said Mr. Revels was involved I told him to come by on Sunday evening.

Sure enough he came about 2 p. m. we removed ourselves to a small cabin that my grandson slept in. W. V. seemed a bit nervous when he started by telling me about things that was happening in the North and that there were white people there that wanted to help organize and protect the former slaves in the South by electing Republicans into office the party of Mr. Lincoln.

He told me that he had personally met with Mr. Revels while visiting Jackson and he was prepared to help organize all colored men from the ages of eighteen to seventy years of age, and any white man who would sign the oath. He told me that the organization was made up of mostly northern white men who believed that the party of Mr. Lincoln must include all colored people because he was the man who freed the slaves.

He said "the organization was called the Loyal League, and he had agreed to head the part that would be formed in Jasper County, he said that if I and my son William would join it was make a big difference in the number of men who would follow. I told him to come back next Sunday, and I would give him my decision.

I told Hannah the reason why W.V. had come and asked her what she thought I should do. She told me to think about it but added that if Mr. Ellis had sent him it must be alright. The following week the Chapter of the Jasper County Loyal League started.

Word spread like a forest fire I could see knowing looks of hope and pride when I saw my neighbors and friends; we never spoke about it in public because it was a secret organization and the fear of night riders who had renewed visiting the homes of colored people was ever present.

Some members had already been "jumped" into the league; they would shake your hand but there was something different in the way that they shook my hand and said a word that I didn't understand. At the time, W. V. asked me to wait until we had our first big meeting before William and I took the oath.

Many of the first big meetings were held on my farm but before the first meeting that brought men from all over Jasper County some of the younger men marched through Paulding singing Yankee songs and having a good time. I advised against such open acts of defiance but the young bucks insisted on doing it. Their foolish show of pride would later cause us more trouble than we could handle. As far as I can remember every eligible colored man joined and a few white men. W. V. McKnight was the leader.

At first we were mostly concerned as to who was going to hold office. William was the first of our children to go off to college at Louisiana State College for Colored Boys. He wanted to study agriculture even though we had enough money to pay for his education Mr. Revels arranged for him to attend on a land grant.

I remember years later when William came back from school in New Orleans he was excited because my name was mentioned in a document that recorded an eye witness account about the Loyal League of Jasper County, Mississippi.

I remember I was sitting on the front porch when he ran up to me. His eyes were wide and full of pride. His voice swelled with pride as he flopped down at my feet and said Paw, tell me all about it. I told him to read the paper to me and when he had finished I said that the story told most of the things that happened that night.

I knew that Mr. Hardy, the lawyer who I began to fix medicine for was going to write an article about the Loyal League of Jasper County because he came to see me and gave me a paper that he was going to send to the white university in Oxford. He said that it was going to be put in the history of Mississippi. He added that since he was going to use my name he wanted me to read it before he completed the story. I had no idea that my son would read it years later.

I did not see Mr. Hardy again until he came to show me the completed Article that he was sending to the university. When he arrived the first thing that I asked him was what happened to W. V. McKnight, that I had not seen him after the meeting at my house?

He simply looked down at the ground and in a low voice and said, "Some things are best to be left alone." I wondered if he knew that I had been there the night and witnessed the first blood bath that took place in Jasper County. Some facts handed down by Cruise family members are not found in the documented recollection of Mr. Hardy.

The following is a written verbatim report of the events in Jasper County as reported in the Mississippi Historical Society Record Vol. IV, circa 1902 by W. H. Hardy.

(Author's Note: the phrases, and dialect, and spacing are in their original format reported in The Mississippi Historical Society Record Vol. IV, circa 1902.)

The Loyal League was a secret, oath-bound organization
and lodges were organized all over the country and every male

Negro from eighteen to seventy years old, and every white man

who would take the oath, was eligible to membership.

Only a few white men became members, but nearly all the male

Negroes within the ages stated, were initiated into its mysteries.

The initiation was to the negro, very solemn and impressive.

They usually met on Saturday night at the cabin of some prominent

negro, or in some vacant outhouse.

Armed sentinels were posted on all the approaches to the house.

In the centre of the room, which was rarely capable of holding one

fourth of the number assembled, was placed a table, or old

goods box, on the centre of which rested an open Bible, and

a deep dish or saucer filled with alcohol and myrrh which was

lighted; above this altar, so-called, was suspended a United

States flag, and also a sword.

The candidate was blindfolded outside and was led in by the arm

And required to kneel at this "altar" and place his hands upon the
open Bible.

The president of the League called upon the chaplain to pray. He
invoked the divine blessing upon the "poor benighted brother
who was about to pass "from the night of bondage in slavery
into the marvelous life and light of freedom."

Short passages from the account of Moses leading the children of
Israel from Egyptian bondage were then read, when the "candidate
was catechized,

something after this fashion [W. V. McKnight was in charge and
asked the questions, and the candidate was required to repeat the
answers] He asked "What is your name?"

Jim Cruise.

Are you a white or colored man?

A colored man.

Were you born free, or a slave?

A slave.

Are you now a slave or a freedman?

A freedman, thank God!

Who freed you?

Abraham Linkum, bless God!

Who helped him to free you?

The Army and the Publican party.

Who fought to keep you in slavery?

The white people of the south, and the Democratic party.

Who then are your best friends?

The Publican party and northern soldiers.

Whom do you want to hold all the offices in this State and govern?

it, make and execute its laws?

The Publicans, the friends of the poor colored man.

Suppose the Democrats carry the elections and get back into

power, what would become of you and all the colored people in the

State?

We would be put back into slavery. God forbid!

All Amen! and amen!!

Then the oath was given.

"I Jim Cruise, do solemnly swear on the holy Bible, in the presence of God and these witnesses, that I will ever remain true and loyal to the Republican party; that I will always vote the Republican ticket; that I will keep secret all the signs, pass word, and grip of the Loyal League; that I will obey all the laws, rules, resolutions, and commands of the League of which I am a member; that I will forever reverence the name and memory of Abraham Lincoln, the author and father of my freedom, and that I will observe and keep in holy remembrance each anniversary of the Emancipation Proclamation, and that I will teach my children to do so. That I will never knowingly vote for any Democrat for any office lest I be put back into bondage and slavery.

That I will never disclose the name of any member of this League, or of any League of which I may become a member, nor tell the place or meeting of the same; that I will not testify against any member of this, or any Loyal League concerning anything done by the League or its order, or the order of any of its officers.

"For a violation of this oath, or any part of it, for the first offense,

I agree to receive fifty lashes on my bare back; and one hundred

lashes for the second offense; and for the third, to be secretly shot

to death by any member of the League appointed for that purpose,

so help me God!"

The blindfold was then removed and the

following lecture was given:

"My Brother: You have just been brought from the darkness of
bondage and slavery, to the glorious light of freedom. You behold

above you the flag of freedom, beneath whose folds the soldiers of
the Union marched and fought; and the sword, the implement with

which they struck from your hands the chains of slavery, and

made you a free man. You behold on your left, a pot of sweet

incense which constantly rises toward heaven. So let your

gratitude, sweetened with humility, and- strengthened with

courage, ever ascend to God in acknowledgment of the blessings

of freedom."

he was then invested with the grip, sign of recognition, password,

and sign and cry of distress.

The Loyal League of Paulding, Jasper county, met regularly

once a month and was usually attended by one or two hundred

negroes, and on extra occasions as many as four or five hundred

would attend, until an exciting event occurred one

Saturday night which practically tore it apart.

"They met at the house of Jim Cruise, a tall   black negro, who was

a house carpenter,

and possessed above the average intelligence of his race.

His house was on a high hill about a mile from Paulding,

where he still resides, unless he has died within the last two

years. I was introduced to him when he was a slave, he use to make

medicine for my wife, from herbs found in the woods. His owner,

Lennon Ellis, a successful business man, and builder, spoke highly

of him. As the years went by, I understood why. A year or so after

the war, he built two houses and a store for me, the job was done

as well as any I have ever seen.

It was common to see a hundred or more negroes march through

the town on Saturday evening, some of them had guns.

Complaints had been made to the general commanding the

department of these armed assemblages, that the whites were

intimidated, especially the women and children, and unless these

armed meetings of the negroes were suppressed by the authorities,

the whites would organize in self defense, and race conflicts

would ensue. The General promptly issued an order forbidding all

persons to assemble with arms, and ordered the sheriffs to enforce

the order by reading it to such assemblies, and order

them to disperse, and if they refused to do so, to report the

same to the nearest military officer.

Richard Simmons was sheriff of Jasper county, an illiterate,

harmless old man; he lived sixteen or eighteen miles from the court

house, but had a gallant ex-Confederate soldier as his deputy,

Major Q. C. Heidelberg, who was raised in Paulding, and who is

now an honored and useful citizen of the town of Heidelberg, on

the New Orleans, and Northeastern Railroad. He desired to break

up these armed meetings and had often remonstrated with the

leaders, but to no purpose; but when he received the order from

the military commander of the district he summoned three

young men, Walter and George Acker and J. W. T. Lambeth

to accompany him one Saturday night to locate the place of

the meeting, and to read the order to the meeting, and warn

them not to bring arms again. He and his posse went to several

places where it had been reported these meetings were

being held but failed to find them, and concluded to return to

town. They were traveling on foot along a narrow lane, the

moon was shining brightly, and suddenly a negro stepped out

from the fence comer with a gun in his hand and shouted,

"halt!" They stopped. The sentinel called out, "Who comes

thar?" Major Heidelberg replied, "I am the deputy sheriff of

the county. Who are you?" The negro gave his name, and

Major Heidelberg commenced to advance, and the negro level-

ed his gun and told him to stop. Major Heidelberg knew the

negro and called him by name, and remonstrated with him, all

the while he and his posse were slowly advancing with their pistols

in their hands, until within ten or twelve paces, when they

covered him, and ordered him to put his gun down, which he

promptly did. They learned from him that the meeting was

then in session at the house of Jim Cruise, about two hundred

yards further down the road. He said he was a picket, put

out there to prevent anybody from coming to the meeting who

didn't have the countersign. The Major told him what his object

was, to promulgate the order against armed assemblies,

and that he must not attend any more meetings armed; and

some of the posse warned him, in language more forceful than

elegant of what he might expect if they caught him again armed.

The negro was thoroughly alarmed and promised obedience,

and the party passed on. When they came opposite

the house the yard swarmed with negroes like black birds on a

hayrick. They could see through the cracks of the building

that it was lighted. They stood in the shadow of a tree and

watched for some time, and they could see persons coming out

and going into the house constantly. There were so many of

them they hesitated to venture up to the house, but determined

to pass on by, and secrete themselves on the roadside in

the hope that they might catch some prominent negro coming

or going, and get further information, or open negotiations.

When past the house about a hundred yards and descending

the hill on which it stood, they were promptly challenged again,

and this time by a more determined negro, but one of the

posse, taking advantage of the animated colloquy between the

deputy sheriff and the negro, made a slight flank movement,

and got close enough to cover him with his pistol, and he laid

his gun down. They learned from him that W. V. McKnight, a

white native, was at the head of the League and was then in the

house and that a great many new members were there from all over

the county to be "tuck in" that night; that there were. Four or five

hundred people were there. The deputy sheriff was urged by two of

his posse to return and break up the meeting.

The negro sentinel urged them not to attempt it. He said fully

half of them were armed, and if they went up there, they could

possibly be killed before McKnight could prevent it. He said that

he would go up and see McKnight, and tell him to come out and see them. This was agreed to, and the negro started in a

brisk walk up the hill, but before getting halfway to the house

a crowd rushed out of the house and yard shouting, "halt those

men! stop those men! shoot those men !" and they came pelmel

down the hill. The deputy sheriff and his posse ran in a

stooping posture to a little thicket near the roadside, and as

they were seen running, the bloodthirsty villains opened fire

on them, and fully twenty or thirty shots were fired; after the

first volley the boys opened on the pursuers with their pistols,

and they not only stopped the pursuit, but the cowardly negroes

scampered back up the hill. A man ran out of the house, and

with a stentorian voice was heard from the house

shouting "stop dat shootin' ! stop dat shootin' !

nobody tole you to shoot."

George Acker and Lambeth were thoroughly enraged by this

time and urged the deputy sheriff that they go back and "clean

out the whole cowardly crew." Major Heidelberg and Walter

Acker, both ex-Confederate soldiers, and as brave and fearless as ever fought under the Southern cross, said, "no, we can run

the whole crowd off, but we would have to kill some of them,

and this we want to avoid, unless they follow us up." So they

walked leisurely on toward the little village of Paulding. They

had gone only a short distance, when someone was seen coming

rapidly toward them. They stepped to one side and lay

down. When he came up they halted him, at the same time

covering him with their pistols. He had a double-barreled

shot-gun in his hand and was scared nearly to death, and

begged piteously that they would not kill him. They were

amazed to find that their prisoner was Thornton Fox, a negro

who had been raised in or near Paulding by Burkitt Lassiter,

the old sheriff, and lived in Paulding, and swept out the sheriff's

office every morning. He had heard the firing and his wife

made him get his gun and commanded him to "run for dear life

and shoot ever white man you see; ef you don' do it I never

will lib wid you anuder day." This was old Thornton's story,

and doubtless was true, for he was a kind-hearted negro, indolent and lazy, worked only at little jobs about town, whilst

his wife was a quarrelsome old virago and a "white folks hater."

"I jes' hates de groun' white fokes walks on, I dus, but thank

God, de bottum rail's on top and the cullud fokes is gwine ter

hab der day now," was a common remark of her's.

Old Thornton was arrested and brought back by the party.

The writer had heard the shooting and knew what it meant,

and with a double-barreled gun and a six shooter, sat near the

front gate of his residence, whilst his wife in fear, watched the

little ones who slept, awaiting tidings from the front. Soon

Major Heidelberg and his party, with Thornton Fox as a

prisoner, came up and a counsel was held as to what was best

to do. Four or five hundred negroes incensed and with revenge in

their hearts, and believing they would be upheld by

the military authorities, might march upon the town and fire

it and commit other and greater crimes against the white women

and children. When asked what was to be done with

Thornton Fox, Major Heidelberg said, "I am going to lock him up in jail. " Lambeth said, "kill him, d n him." George

Acker said, "say the word, Major, and I will shoot the infamous

scoundrel now!" The negro was thoroughly overcome with

fear, and prostrated himself upon the ground and begged for

his life, and laid all the blame on his wife. It was finally agreed

to keep Thornton's gun and send him back on parole to the

League, and find out what was going on; whether they proposed

to attack the town or not, and report back within one

hour, at the outside. He was thoroughly alarmed, and left on

a run and within thirty minutes was back and reported that the

meeting had "done broke up and the niggers was all skeered,

and was leavin' in all directions for home." He further reported

that W. V. McKnight, the white man who was at the

head of the League, was greatly alarmed, and that he had selected

over one hundred armed negroes to accompany him home. He had

gone through the woods and fields, avoiding the roads.

At the next term of the circuit court the district attorney was

absent and the writer was appointed district attorney, pro tern.

The grand jury indicted eight or ten of the leaders for conspiracy. The next term was 'pretermitted', and in the meantime Jonathan Tarbell, a carpet-bagger from the State of New York, had been appointed circuit judge, and Simon Jones, a scallawag, of Brandon, had been appointed district attorney. When the conspiracy cases were reached the district attorney arose and stated that the cases were purely political, that no offense had been committed against the laws of the State, and entered a nolle pros equi."

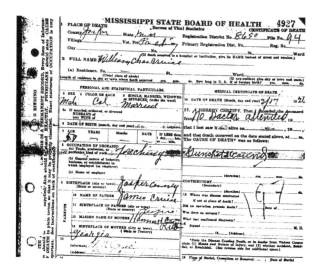

MISSISSIPPI STATE BOARD OF HEALTH 4927
Bureau of Vital Statistics
CERTIFICATE OF DEATH

1 PLACE OF DEATH
County Jasper State Miss Registration District No. 8650 File No. 94
Village Vot. Pct. Paulding Primary Registration Dist. No. Reg. No.
City No. St. Ward
2 FULL NAME William Chas Cruise
(a) Residence. No. St. Ward.

PERSONAL AND STATISTICAL PARTICULARS
3 SEX Male 4 COLOR OR RACE Col. 5 SINGLE, MARRIED, WIDOWED OR DIVORCED (write the word) Married
8 DATE OF BIRTH (month, day and year)
7 AGE 57 YEARS
8 OCCUPATION OF DECEASED (a) Trade, profession, or particular kind of work Teaching
9 BIRTHPLACE (city or town) (State or country) Jasper County
10 NAME OF FATHER James Cruise
11 BIRTHPLACE OF FATHER (city or town) (State or country) Georgia
12 MAIDEN NAME OF MOTHER Hannah [illegible]
13 BIRTHPLACE OF MOTHER (City or town) (State or Country) Georgia
Informant
(Address)

MEDICAL CERTIFICATE OF DEATH
16 DATE OF DEATH (Month, day and year) 3/17 19 26
17. I HEREBY CERTIFY, That I attended the deceased from No Doctor attended, 19
that I last saw h alive on, 19
and that death occurred on the date stated above, at m.
The CAUSE OF DEATH* was as follows:
Gunshot wound
(duration) yrs. mos. ds.
CONTRIBUTORY (Secondary)
Signed M.D.
18 Place of Burial, Cremation or Removal Date of Burial

STATE OF MISSISSIPPI
STATE BOARD OF HEALTH
Bureau of Vital Statistics
CERTIFICATE OF DEATH

1 PLACE OF DEATH
County Jones
Inc. Town or Village Ellisville Registration District No. 422 File No. 757
Primary Registration District No. 2314 Registered No. 16
2 FULL NAME Josiah Cruise

PERSONAL AND STATISTICAL PARTICULARS
3 SEX Male 4 COLOR OR RACE Colored 5 SINGLE, MARRIED, WIDOWED, OR DIVORCED Wid.
6 DATE OF BIRTH Nov. 26, 1812
7 AGE 100 yrs. mos. 1 ds.
8 OCCUPATION Mechanic
9 BIRTHPLACE (State or Country) Ga.
10 NAME OF FATHER Charles Cruise
11 BIRTHPLACE OF FATHER (State or Country) Ga.
12 MAIDEN NAME OF MOTHER Nellie Adams
13 BIRTHPLACE OF MOTHER (State or Country) Ga.
14 THE ABOVE IS TRUE TO THE BEST OF MY KNOWLEDGE
(Informant) J. Henry Cruise
(Address) Paulding Miss
15 Filed Nov. 24 1912 A. J. Carter Registrar

MEDICAL CERTIFICATE OF DEATH
16 DATE OF DEATH Nov. 24, 1912
17 I HEREBY CERTIFY, That I attended the deceased from Nov. 11th 1912, to Nov. 24, 1912, that I last saw him alive on Nov. 17th, 1912, and that death occurred on the date stated above, at 2 p.m.
The CAUSE OF DEATH* was as follows:
Senile Insanity
Duration yrs. mos. 14 ds.
Contributory
Signed A. J. Carter M.D.
Nov. 24 1912 Address Ellisville Miss
19 PLACE OF BURIAL OR REMOVAL Paulding Miss DATE OF REMOVAL Nov. 24 1912
20 UNDERTAKER J. Henry Cruise ADDRESS Paulding
Form V. S. No. 4.

CHAPTER 9

A BLOOD BATH

There were other families who bear mentioning, some for good and others for deeds that did not help the colored people. Other than the whites who helped, was the Hosey, the Ellis, and Foggy families, and also Thornton Fox who told the white folks everything he heard that the colored folks were doing.

In fact, on the night of the shooting we told him that we were going to meet in one or two possible places on that eventful Saturday night. He told the Deputy Sheriff but when they went to the places he told them where we were meeting, they did not find us.

Some years later around 1893, Thornton Fox worked under me in a road gang when the county began to hire a few colored men to repair and pave the roads. (See pg. 164)

He knew that I was aware that he was behind a lot of things the white people were doing to colored people especially how he was involved the time that the shooting started on my farm. He was always uneasy around me but I never took any action according to the rules of the league because I could have ordered some member to kill him or could have killed him myself because he gave out the names of some members of the Loyal League. Instead of killing him, I forgave him and prayed for him.

When the shooting had stopped that Saturday night, I ran to the house to check on Hannah and the children, because bullets were flying everywhere. I found them hiding in our secret place; I told her that W. V. had left for home with about fifty armed men went with him because he was afraid for his life. I was going to see about him and his family and I told her not to come out from our hiding place until I got back.

I took Richard Foggy and started for the McKnight place; it was about two miles from my farm. We took the path near the edge of the woods and although we could not see anyone; as we came closer to his house we could hear gunfire and the sound of a lot of horses. That dark feeling from long ago hit me in my stomach.

When we reached the clearing I had no idea that I was about to see The Blood Bath In Jasper County, Mississippi was unfolding before our eyes. I heard screaming and as I looked to my left I saw horses trampling who appeared to be two of the McKnight children. In the clearing just beyond the house, I saw several colored men that had already been strung up to a low hanging tree. Although they were already dead some of the riders continued to beat them with bull whips. There was nothing really left of their backs except bones. There was little or no skin. As we circled for a closer look we could see puddles of blood everywhere.

About fifty yards to my right men on horses were firing into a line of colored men, boys really, who had never been up that late let alone been in any type of gun play. They were slaughtered one after another and people were running in every which a way.

At first it looked like they were trying to run away, but what they were doing was trying to help their fallen family members and the men who had left the meeting with W.V. but they didn't know who to help first.

When I saw W. V. there were about five men on horseback who had formed a circle and in the middle of the circle, he was being beaten like a wild dog. They were kicking him in the face and calling him names he kind of went from horse, to horse, being tossed about like a busted sack of potatoes.

Finally he went to the ground at which time the riders rode over him time and again mashing his body into the earth. The things that we witnessed that night will never escape from my mind. When the rest of the McKnight family saw what was happening to W. V. they began to run from the house the men started to shoot them one by one. None of the McKnight family made it ten yards from the porch. Two of the boys were shot before they could reach the bottom of the stairs.

I believe his mother was killed when one of the men on horseback threw a rope around her neck, and dragged her off into the woods. We sat there and could not believe what was happening. I wanted to scream for help to try and save them but Richard pulled me back down and said, "Not even God can help us now." We retreated further into the woods realizing that we could do nothing to help. By the time the sun came up none of the McKnight family or any member of the league who went with him was left alive.

All we could do was watch in horror. I still shake even today as I remember that horrible night. We did not stay to see what happened to the bodies but when I returned two days later there was no sign that anything had ever happened. I have not seen any of them again. There were no bodies no charred building that remained; not a sign that a struggle ever happened or that a house had ever sat on the property. Every inch of that land had been dug up and turned over as if ready for planting.

I know for sure that there were twelve colored men from Paulding who never returned home from that fateful night. Richard and I have never talked about what we saw that night; I don't think we ever wanted to. Every time I think of that night and I have often, I get so far, and my mind just goes blank.

Government men came to Jasper County about 1905, and found that there was oil beneath the ground, but they could not get to it because it was so deep. Very few colored people knew how this would affect them but William explained it to me that whoever first owned the ground owned the rights to what was below it. He called it sub surface rights.

Things began to change for the worst for colored people who owned land, if things could get any worst. Night riders started to come by every week. We all knew who they were by their voices and by the horses that they were riding. At first they would yell out curses and threats and would tell us to get off of the land.

They would make loud noises and would shoot into the air. They started to burn crosses near the houses, and to throw rocks on the tin roofs. Instead of running to the woods when they came by we dug out the remainder of the kitchen floor and shored it up with timber making it the same size of the kitchen. I built a false wall that concealed the drop door leading to the room below.

We added even more smoked meat and a lot of water. I put the meat in the box that I made for the corner of the room. Although the meat was smoked, Hannah would change it out and cook it and replace some recently smoked meat in the box. The room was now big enough for the whole family. Our plan was to go into the lower room if the Klan came to burn down our house. I knew first hand that if they sat fire to the house and we ran out they would shoot my whole family. We practiced getting into that hole every week because their visits became more frequent.

CHAPTER 10

THE BLACK CODE

I stopped building houses mostly because the white folks quit hiring me. Mr. Ellis had moved to Jones County, and since he was no longer lived in Jasper County he could not sign a work permit for me to work even if I got a job.

He would come by about every two months on his way to his business in Laurel he was now involved in with a Mr. Gardner in the lumber business.

He told me that things were getting bad all over the county so much so that some people began to lose their lives. He was the first person to tell me about the Black Code, a set of laws aimed at putting colored people back into bondage by taking away their right to vote and many other laws that made it look as if we were lazy and needed to be put back in slavery.

You had to have some white man sign for you to get a permit to work unless of course, you owned your own land and did nothing but farm. I had a meeting with my sons and reminded them of the oath that I had taken on that fateful night when I joined the Loyal League. I told them that if real trouble started they were to leave Mississippi and never come back; but they should never sell the land.

I told them to stay together as a family because family is all you have and when times got hard they would need each other, no matter where they went. Mr. Ellis came to ask me to move to Ellisville. He said that "I would be able to work as much as I wanted because he was building a lot of houses in Jones and Smith counties. I thanked him and asked if he would continue to buy timber from me. He ordered one thousand feet both smooth and rough side. We agreed to deliver the timber within the next thirty days. He wanted to pay me in advance for the first load but I told him that I still had some of the money that I had made ten years ago; by this time gold was hard for anybody to get. I told him the men working with me would wait until the timber was delivered.

I made an agreement with Robert Hosey and Richard Foggy to help cut the trees for the railroad and skin the timber for cabinets. As always Mr. Ellis was fair with me and I was able to pay them a good wage for their labor.

I paid them three dollars a day for a ten hour day, more than most folks made in those days in a week, colored or white. My sons and daughters began to have children and by this time colored children went to school. William was one of the school teachers at Spring Hill School located about two miles Southeast of Paulding.

I continued to get visits from the Klan from time to time, and many dirty looks but I believe the reason that the Klan did not visit more often, was due to the influence that Mr. Ellis still had in Jasper County. I also believe that he and Mr. Hardy, kept an eye on me from a distance and it was definitely by the grace of God!

I never borrowed any money on my land but I gave William, Joseph and Hiram forty acres each and kept forty for myself. I was happy to see my children and grand children growing up to be good citizens, and getting an education; all of them did not go to college but it was not because they couldn't afford to. William and Joseph were the only boys who graduated from college, one from Louisiana State College, and Joseph from Alcorn, where my old friend Hiram Revels was the president and a Methodist Minister.

As far as anybody else knew, I was still working for Mr. Ellis after he had moved to Jones County. He continued to not only build houses in Smith and Jones Counties, but was part owner in a business of digging up clay and making it into bricks just outside of Paulding.

Things were still hard for colored people; but being free compared with being a slave was the difference between night and day. When William returned from college he began teaching at one of the two colored schools. He moved to the Spring Hill School because many of his students were his "close kin" or families that he grew up with. The Hosey children, the Foggy family, my son Hiram and Anderson Lee, Sye Lee's grandson all went to school together.

As I watched the sunset over what I believe to be my final days, I feel that I have lived a good and full life. Yes, I was born a slave but I shall die a free man. If there is anything that I would change about my life it would be that I would have died before my dear Hannah. But knowing she died happy in the Lord, gives comfort to my soul.

I never want anyone to know what it was like being a slave. I pray to God that everyone will always breathe free air, and be able to take ownership for themselves and their family. I think that I have raised my family well. I have taught them to be strong for themselves, for their children, and for all of our people and to always remember that it was God that brought us all through the wilderness of slavery.

I know that the white men who owned slaves will never give up the idea of ownership. Although we won a battle the war will continue to be fought through laws that will bind our hands and feet tighter than the ropes that held us in bondage that kept us as slaves. Our new slavery will be in the form of ignorance, distrust of each other and the lack of information about our homeland and our family history. We must never lose sight of the fact that we are from Africa and until we learn of our people and their contribution to their time and place, we cannot escape the bondage of self, that ask, who are you, and why are you the person that you are. Black men must prove the slave master wrong who instilled in our women that we are not men who provided for the safety and well being of our families and our community. America has perfected the ability to condemn the world while committing the same acts of oppression to the people who slaved for two hundred years to make it the great leader of the so called free world.

The colored man has always wanted to trust the white man who is in his best state. I have been blessed to know some who in spite of what the masses did, stood up for justice and goodness. Two such men I met as a young man, Mr. Ellis and W. V. McKnight, the other was Marsh Cook who I met around 1880, in fact he was one of the white men who signed the oath of the Loyal League; he was killed by the Klan for educating colored people about voting and the importance of voting for the Republican party.

I am sure that things that happen in one generation will happen in a generation to come. Colored people will become tenants of the new plantation and find themselves living at the lowest levels of community life. Change will come for us, but this change must come through leadership from within those communities.

PART 2

CHAPTER 11

LIFE ON THE HILL

My name is Hiram Revels Cruise. This is my story…This is our story…This is the way life was and I am glad that we lived it. Many who know me would think that I would be the last choice to tell our family's story because I am quiet and keep to myself; but I feel that I was chosen by my father to tell it.

Life on what we called "the hill" was both interesting and adventurous. Although our family worked hard we always took time to play. My father James would always say, "All work and little or no play would not lead to happiness."

We discovered ways to entertain ourselves with whatever we could find. And, we had plenty of room to wander, I remember one day when my brother Frank started a game he called catch me if you can; we ran as fast as we could hiding among the thick trees that surrounded our property. But, no matter how hard we tried Frank would always find us.

And, we never hungered for food; it just grew every place on our farm. Joseph was two years older than me, he always had a hard time keeping up because he was short plus he always stopped to eat wild blue berries that ran along the path. There were apples, peaches, wild berries, figs and pecans. Often, we just ate the fruit from our trees, and berries by the buckets.

Our daily challenge was to find new adventures that the next day would bring. Our father gave us the run of the place but we were never to go further than the creek, which ran about a mile deep into the woods. Frank, Tommie, Joseph and I knew every inch of that land like the back of our hands.

On special occasions my father would take us deep into the woods even sometime beyond the creek, he taught us to recognize the different plants that could be used to help make people well. I learned the art well, and I was able to teach my sons the same thing.

Although my name is Hiram my father James called me "Dib" because that's what I am. I am very deliberate in everything that I do. I was born in Jasper County, Mississippi on January 3, 1877. I want to continue the story of my families' rich, and sometime tragic history. I will tell it with truth, I tell it with honesty, and I will tell it deliberately after all that is why they call me "Dib."

My father James died the day before Thanksgiving, in 1912. When we had his funeral it seemed like all of Jasper County attended. It was a bitter sweet day in our life, I cried tears of joy, sadness, pain and relief because he suffered and was in great pain for three months before he died. He seldom knew who he was, or recognized anybody, and we believed that he would again be with his beloved Hannah.

We sent a great man home that day; he took a part of us with him but he left us much more than gold or silver could buy…our good name. Because of my father James I am proud to carry the name and I hope that I can be half the man that he was.

My mother Hannah Reid Cruise died February 14, 1909. It was a sad day for all of us. She was the rib bone, the heart, the spirit, and soul of the Cruise family.

My father took her death very hard. Even though he never let us see him cry I would catch him sometimes standing under an old oak tree in Paulding near the newly build white church speaking as though he was talking to my mother. In fact, it was under this same tree where they first met privately, and where he asked her to marry him.

Even though I started my story talking about death, this is a story about life, more than it is about people dying. From my earliest memories I want to say that our life was about learning; our parents had one goal in mind, to help us become the best that we could be. Not, only book learning but they taught us about God. The first thing I learned was how to pray, then I learned my A B C's...

One of my fondest memories as a child was eating sweet cane, and singing A B C D E F G... I can remember sitting in my mother's lap, as my sisters' Amanda and Harriet (Hattie) combed my mother's long beautiful black hair; it was the color of coal. They would alternate singing school and church songs to me. So, in our house God and education went "hand in hand."

My father told us that he learned to read from the Holy Bible. It was given to him by a white man whom he said was his friend, a Mr. Lennon Ellis. My oldest sister Mary told us that he was a man who had owned our family as slaves.

As I look back I realize what great love I have always had for my family, how proud I am of each and every one of them. I could never truly put into words how I feel and what it means to be a Cruise. I have always tried to instill this sense of well-being into my children.

Although we had been taught a lot at home when we started my formal education I was so proud of the fact that my first school teacher was my brother William. He had gone to college in the big city of New Orleans. He was in every sense to me a true hero. I wanted to make him and all of my family especially proud of me.

We were taught the difference between right and wrong and to always tell the truth at a very early age. So I say this with a pure and simple heart the first time that I saw Gertrude Foggy I knew that she would someday be my wife. She was my schoolmate and the daughter of my father's best friend; I told her so when I was just eight years old.

She smiled, and as she ran away, she fell and skinned her knee. I walked her home that day. I carried her book while knowing in my heart what God had given to me, and that we would spend the rest of our lives together.

The next few years went by quickly for me, in part because I enjoyed learning, and secondly I sat next to Gertrude who by this time was planning our wedding every day. I felt as if I have always known her, and actually, I have. She would go on and on about who would stand where, what kind of flowers they would carry, putting this person in the wedding and the next day taking that person out.

My father asked me if I wanted to attend college. After thinking it over I realized that I could not be any further from Gertrude than the distance between her house and mine. I told my father that I wanted to raise cows and pigs and become a butcher. I went on to say that I would be able to take care of a family from the money that I earned.

He seemed surprised but by this time everyone in the family knew that I was set on marrying Gertrude. I think he was proud of me, and he knew I would make a good father, husband, and family man.

He often told me how he had virtually saved every penny that he had been paid as a young man. I think he admired that quality in me as well as in my brothers. Even though he never told us what to do with our money he instilled in us the value of having money and owning our own land. We knew that he never wanted us to give up or sell our land.

I remember the day when I went to ask Gertrude's father for her hand in marriage. Frank and Tommie went with me laughing all the way. Afterwards they told everyone that they had to hold me up because I kept stumbling along and they were afraid that I would fall and mess up my one good suit.

When we arrived at the Foggy's farm Gertrude's father was sitting on the porch. He stood as I came up the three steps that seemed like I was climbing a mountain. When I stumbled at the top step Frank and Tommie had to catch me to keep me from falling.

The laughing had stopped and all of a sudden everyone was serious. I didn't know whether to stay or run. Then I saw Gertrude standing in the doorway. Suddenly, I had the confidence of a "Cock Rooster." I reached out to shake Mr. Foggy's hand; he put his arm around my shoulder and said, "Boy, what took you so long."

He went on to say, "We have been family from the first day that I first met your father." He reminded me of the time I came to visit Gertrude during a bad rain storm and how I refused to remove my rain coat. When he told my father about this incident, my father told him that I was so desperate to see Gertrude that I went dressed only in hip boots and a raincoat.

I never knew that it took so much planning just to "jump the broom." So I learned to just look down and say "yes dear" to whatever she said; a saying that has served me well over the years

Finally, the day arrived that Gertrude had long talked about and planned for; the day that I had long dreamed about and had foreseen years ago. It was nothing like we thought it would be. It was more than we had ever dreamed it could be. It seemed as though it was not just our wedding, but the wedding of all of Jasper County's colored people, and some whites. The whole town showed up. From the time I saw Gertrude in her white dress I couldn't take my eyes off of her; her skin was the color of fresh hay; she was as fair as the sun.

We were married on the hill overlooking Paulding. For some reason my father made sure that I rode up the hill from the bottom land riding on a big mule. As I passed a few of the white guests I remembered what my father had said about colored men riding on mules. Things were looking up!

True to form I was nervous as the day is long. That was until I saw my bride. She was in a simple white dress which made her more beautiful than a field of wild flowers in the springtime; her long beautiful black hair made her dress look like an angel's robe, her veil could not hide her beauty.

We both shed tears of joy as did both our families. It seemed like an eternity but my brother Joseph who was our local preacher married us in less than ten minutes including our jumping the broom.

The women from both sides of the family had been preparing food for at least a week. I don't think that there was a chicken in Paulding that was left un-fried, or a berry in Jasper County that wasn't in a pie. It truly was the happiest day of our lives. It was the beginning of a new family who resided on the hill. I can truly say for one day, there was peace on earth.

The fruit of our union produced sixteen children; they were all born healthy with the exception of one son who was still born. But to my father the most important thing was that most of his children and all of his grand children were born as free people.

CHAPTER 12

STRAWS FROM THE BROOM

God blessed us with our first child in 1897. We named him William after my brother. Gertrude and I looked up to him because he was our teacher and in part because he played a major role in bringing the two of us together. He was a leading citizen in Paulding and a great role model for any man colored or white.

The turn of the century brought little relief for colored men in the South. Things seemed especially hard for us in Jasper County. The Black Code had been perfected and most colored people stopped voting because of the Poll Tax Law. Colored people felt the full force of the Klan and the intimidating and the murderous ways that had become the normal way they operated.

Colored people had to look out for themselves. There was no longer any Loyal League to help. There was nothing left to be loyal to because the Republican Party had traded us in because of politics at least twenty years before when they passed the compromise bill around 1877.

It seemed as though many white folks blamed colored people for anything bad that happened to them. If they had no land it was the fault of the colored. If they had no food it was the fault of colored people. Some went so far to say, "If God didn't answer their prayers it was because He was busy answering the prayer of the colored people. We thought that part to be true because God only answers true and just prayers.

Horrible things; unspeakable things were happening all over the county. We always had to be three steps ahead of the white people;

in many ways we had figured them out long before they could figure out what they wanted to do.

We just could not meet their rage and their ignorance in their treatment of colored people. We wanted peace and to be left alone; they wanted blood and the land that we owned. We wanted to work for what we had; they wanted to take it from us and destroy us and our family values.

Only God knows why they wanted revenge. Revenge for what? Because colored people were no longer slaves? It makes no sense after all we were the people who were brought here against our will. Our families had often discussed these things trying to figure out why things were happening this way. Harriet would often say, "How do you reason with a savage?"

Most white men did a double take when they saw me and Gertrude together, as if they were thinking what is that "darkey" doing with that pretty white woman; lucky for me, most of them knew that she was a mulatto and because I was a Cruise which meant something around these parts, but I could still feel the hate in their eyes.

For this reason I made sure that Gertrude and I were seldom together in town except when we went through town to church. I never let Gertrude and little William go to town alone.

Our second, Harriet (we called her Hattie after my sister) was born in the fall of 1899, she was like her mother a very pretty child. My son William (we called him Henry) acted as if she was his child; he wanted to hold her but Gertrude would only let him touch her.

My older brother Joseph was a big help when I started to buy my first stock; he had a natural talent for raising cows and pigs, plus he had taken farming courses in college.

After my father was satisfied that I wanted to start my own business he loaned me four hundred dollars and gave me forty acres of land. I was always a serious family man and one thing that I took pride in was that along with my Father and my older brothers, we made sure that our sisters were taken care of. My sisters all married good men who believed in God, hard work and providing for their family.

Gertrude and I started out working hard. We would get up at day break, feed the animals and tend to the garden, and I would go and work in the field where I had planted feed for the pigs and the prized bull that I bought from a farmer in Jones County.

Our family got together at least twice a month. By this time all of my brothers were married and the only one missing was Frank who was sent to prison because he defended himself by hitting a white man who was attempting to beat him with a whip.

After serving five years and with the help of my brothers William Charles and Joseph Henry, my brother Frank was pardoned from prison in the summer of 1903 and was ordered to leave Mississippi. We have never heard from him since his release. It was reported that he moved to Chicago and later worked with Al Capone as his bodyguard.

During the first two years of our marriage I did not try to sell any meat to white people. In fact, I sold most of my beef to my family and friends. "Unbeknowest" to me The Black Code was not being enforced as hard as it had been in the past. After talking with William and Joseph they convinced me to send a letter to the newspaper announcing I would be in town to sell meat on Saturday; it cost me five cents for the announcement. I made enough money that year to buy another 120 acres of land.

Three years later when my son William Henry started to school my brother William Charles was still teaching, but he had moved to the Spring Hill School. Gertrude and I decided to send our children there because we knew that they would get a good education. I can't say that Henry liked the idea of his uncle being his teacher.

After a few days he said that he felt good that his teacher had the same name as his. Henry was a good student and had to earn every grade that he got. My brother William may have been extra hard on him I know that he was with me and Gertrude because he never wanted anyone to say that we did not earn our grades.

Henry always said that he wanted to be a doctor. The only white doctor who would see colored people was Dr. Carter; he would encourage Henry when he had the occasion to visit us. Dr. Carter moved to Ellisville in the spring of 1902, in fact he was my father's doctor and was the one who signed his death certificate in November of 1912.

Trouble really started in Paulding and Heidelberg after oil was discovered by the people from the government Land Bureau while they were conducting surveys in 1906. One of the first places that oil was discovered was on land owned by Sye Lee. I knew the family well and my son William Henry had gone to school with Anderson Lee, Sye Lee's oldest son.

Life in Paulding had become an uneasy dance for Colored folks. For the first time you could say that true segregation had become the order of life. Never before had colored and whites acted so separately; at first colored stores thrived and colored people were self sufficient, but through intimidation and unjust laws we began to lose hope and many wanted to move up north.

It wasn't until the horror of hate and resentment of the ignorant began to raise its ugly head. The Klu Klux Klan was bent on destroying any success for any colored persons. They increased the number of night rides, house burnings, and total intimidation.

We spent most of our time defending ourselves and our love ones from the enemy from within; building and re-building our homes and our businesses. Some left for the North, unfortunately in some cases we buried good men whose only crime was being colored.

I helped so many families pack and say goodbye; some went North some to the Delta, and some to God knows where. Because of the times I had to be more deliberate with my children than I wanted; what I taught them was centered on survival in a white man's world.

They had to know how to survive off the land; so I took them to the woods and showed them how to learn directions by looking at the moss on the side of a tree. I taught them which berries were good to eat, and which ones were poisonous. I taught them how to think on their feet, even the game of hide and go seek had a purpose. I taught them how to survive, and to use everything they could to their advantage. I also took this time to teach them how to identify different roots and herbs and how to cook them and make medicine the same as my father taught me. William seemed to catch on faster than the others.

Gertrude taught the girls the art of mixing the different herbs for different sicknesses. My mother's health took a turn for the worse around the end of 1907, we tried every medicine that we knew of; we even took her to Dr. Carter but he could not find out what was wrong with her.

She died peacefully holding my father's hand, in 1909. As we stood around her bed, holding each others' hands we prayed for our father because we knew that her death was going to take a lot out of him.

Winter was setting in and the ground would be hard in a week or so. My brother Joseph who had recently become an undertaker took care of everything. I am still amazed how he seemed to detach himself from the whole thing as he prepared our mother for her final resting place. She was buried in the Spring Hill Cemetery just below the Spring Hill Baptist Church that was founded by Joseph.

CHAPTER 13

MURDER AT THE DIPPING VAT

As I look back I see my mother's death signaling the change of an era. Pain, death and tragedy would become a constant visitor to the family Cruise. After my mother died my father was never quite the same.

Although he never carried my mother's death like a cross, he did carry the pain to his grave. For several years he was cared for by one of his granddaughters, Emma Foggy. He began to go down in the spring of 1910, and he never fully recovered.

After a respectful time there were several widows who made no secret of the fact that they wanted to marry my father. I would often hear him say that he only needed one wife.

After much thought and debate, it was decided that he would move with our sister Alice who lived in nearby Ellisville. Everybody both colored and white knew that Paulding would never be the same. He died on November 24, 1912.

Surprisingly enough Klan activity in Jasper County went on a decline for several months. It was almost as though white people didn't know how to increase Klan intimidation. I don't think it was out of respect for my father's death. But, it could have been they didn't know how colored people would react at being antagonized so soon after his death. My father was well loved and respected by colored and white people.

When the Klan did return to their activities, it was with vengeance. It seemed as though every other night they would visit as many as five or six families trying to intimidate us; burning at least two houses each night. Again, everybody was on edge. I believe that living under this constant pressure indirectly lead to the still birth

97

of our tenth son who we did not give a name. I buried him myself under a lone oak that sat beside our house.

I remember afterwards that I held Gertrude for two whole days never saying a word just rocking her back and forth. It seemed that the days got darker and darker; my brother Joseph told us that he was having some trouble with what he thought were unfair and unwarranted offers for his land and his cattle. In fact, he was surprised because he had no intention of ever selling his land or his live stock.

He said that he was getting visits from the Klan but it was nothing to be worried about, he thought. He couldn't have been more wrong. The day they killed my brother Joseph plays over and over in my mind. For years, I kept thinking if I had only changed this or done that; anyway, these are the facts.

On April 29, 1914 my brother went to the dipping vat to dip his cows in order to keep the flies and insects away. It had been raining for several days and it was the first time I was able to complete some chores on my farm, otherwise we would have gone together as we normally did.

He was shot down in cold blood by a man named Jim O'Flynn who lied and said that my brother did something totally against his nature. My brother was one of the gentlest people you would ever meet. O'Flynn claimed that he shot him because he approached him in a threatening manner with a cow bell that weighted less than three pounds. The coward claimed that he was afraid for his life but everyone knew that O'Flynn was lying and that he was a murderer.

I was working near the wood line clearing some brush when I heard Gertrude's voice hysterically calling my name over and over. I didn't know what had happened, but I knew something was terribly wrong. I dropped my hoe and ran toward her. When I got near to her, I could see the fear and the tears streaming from her eyes. As she fell into my arms as though every bone in her body had been broken she cried out Joseph's name, over and over.

By this time my heart was pounding so hard it sounded like a drum beat to my ears. After about a minute I could make out what she was saying. She was saying, "Joseph, they have killed Joseph." As I held her in my arms I fell to my knees and began to cry.

Everything from that moment until I got to town is still very dark to me. When I got there they had covered my brother's body with a dirty sack cloth. I had to remember the whole time how not to lose my head. I had to do things step by step, the most important thing was first to retrieve my brother's body and take him to his house.

We went to the dipping vat to bring the cows home. By the time we got there the whole family had gathered. We took his body and laid it in the cabin that my father had built years earlier. A short time later the Sheriff and his two deputies came by. One of the deputies kept saying over and over "We don't want no trouble out of you people."

The Sheriff said that although there were no witnesses he had to take O'Flynn's account until it could all be cleared up, he was bringing O'Flynn in. He promised that he would get to the bottom of what happened. I recall that one deputy looked down at the ground and the other just smirked.

One of them was chewing tobacco; the youngest deputy took off his hat as he looked down and said, "I am sorry." The other pushed his hat back from off his forehead and said, "Just remember we don't want any trouble out of you people."

I took two quick steps toward him and he stumbled backwards swallowing his tobacco which made his eyes bulge and tear. I am glad that I caught myself or there would have been another senseless murder on that day and how would that bring Joseph back?

After they left it took me a while to calm down. Gertrude tried to talk to me. William and Anna tried to talk to me, but no one was getting through. Finally, I took one of the old chairs that my father always sat in that he had made for himself.

I took the chair to the cabin where Joseph was laying. I sat next to him until the next day. I would not allow anyone to touch his body until then. I cleaned him up and washed the mud from his body and the dried blood from his chest and from his mouth. I then realized that he was not shot from close range and the bullet, not shotgun pellets had struck him under his left arm pit as though he was turning away. He never had a chance.

O'Flynn was out of jail the next day. He was back at his dipping vat as though nothing had happened. Even though I didn't understand it and I didn't want to accept it a white man could get away with murdering a colored man.

He was never tried or convicted for his crime. He posted bail of two thousand dollars and never saw the inside of a court house because the grand jury refused to indict him.

We wanted to have a small quiet funeral for our brother but that was not the case, as it was with my father. Joseph had touched many lives in his capacity as a preacher, undertaker, and a friend to just about every farmer in the county. He taught many of them how to better use their land to grow crops.

Many people talked about changing things but it seemed to me that things had taken a change for the worse. Although it rained very hard for three days before we buried Joseph it rained even harder on the day that we buried him; it seemed as though people came two by two from every corner of the county to pay their last respects.

It was then that I realized that my brother meant so much, to so many people including our family. I also realized that hate no matter how senseless it is might one day tear this country apart.

I stood with Beulah his wife at the grave side until well after dark. For three days afterwards, Gertrude and I would have to go and bring her back from the cemetery. Joseph's death hurt us all very deeply. After my brother's death some colored folks wanted blood, they wanted to fight back. They felt the only way that they would see justice would be for them to do it themselves, "An eye for an eye."

After all, two generations of colored folks had grown up never knowing what it was to have been a slave. Many of us had no fear of whites and felt we should burn their houses the same way that they had burned ours. I saw no victory in all out war; they were well armed and to well established and quite frankly, I feel they were just more barbaric.

This didn't stop some of the young bucks in our community from wanting to redistribute the hurt. In fact, twice I had to stop William Jr. and my sons Henry and Joel from going to town along with about six other young men who wanted the heads of white men no matter who they were. Many of them were totally frustrated with what was going on in Jasper County.

The Black codes were still in full effect. Although Lincoln had freed the slaves we were still very much second class citizens. And, even though most of us owned our own land white folks wanted us to think that they still owned us.

We heard the thunder and then and there committed ourselves to stopping the storm. It doesn't matter how or when the storm comes but how you handle it when it arrives. I didn't want to see anymore blood or bury anymore bodies colored or white.

About a month after we buried Joseph, William came to see me and said "there are several white ministers from Jasper County who wanted to talk to us about Joseph and the future of the Spring Hill Church." You see since our brother's death it had been William and I who have been serving as the ministers of the Spring Hill Church.

I am not sure how good of a job we had been doing. In my opinion we did not do as well as Joseph had done but we were able to keep the doors open and the people were still coming.

The colored church served as the only place where colored people could go to have their needs taken care of. Some came because they needed food and some came because they needed help with their crops, and many came because they just needed someone to talk to.

A lot of people today don't understand just how hard life was on a person's mind back in those days. I am not saying that people don't have it hard now, but it seems to me that people today just don't realize how hard it was to think things through back then. It was a lot of pressure just trying to make it, just trying to make ends meet; just trying to live life without losing your mind.

If I may just talk for a moment I would like for people to realize that we were second class citizens and the effects of that did some terrible things to a lot people's minds. Remember we were having our houses burned, our women were being raped, and several were having their land taken from them. In many cases we were treated like we were less than human which had a devastating effect on us.

The church was the only place that a colored person could go and "lay their burdens down." I don't know to this day how Joseph could do the work of a minister. He handled a tremendous burden. He was responsible for many lives and souls. Sadly, for a lot of people he was their connection to God, when he died, God died.

Beulah had thrown herself into the work at the church but she still suffered deeply from the loss of her husband. I understood this because I to suffered deeply from the loss of Joseph. I couldn't imagine how I would feel if I had loss my life-mate, the way she had lost hers.

My whole family pitched in trying to help the church wherever we could. As I said, William and I did the preaching; my sons Henry, John and Joel helped people in any way they could. Beulah, Gertrude and my sisters Harriet and Anna visited every family in the congregation when they needed a shoulder to cry on, a word of encouragement or a hand to hold, these wonderful women were always available.

I can never say enough about what they did. Yet still, this was not our life's work and we needed to find someone who could carry on Joseph's dream. We knew that no one could replace him but we had to find someone who could carry on.

So when William said there were white ministers who wanted to meet with us, at first I didn't take it very well. I asked William why they wanted to meet. They hadn't provided us with any help beside the fact that they were a church. There was no connection.

There was no way that a colored congregation was going to have a white minister nor were we going to close the doors of the Spring Hill Church; it was my brother's legacy. I again asked William why, and what did they want?

William said "I am not sure of everything they want, and he assured me that it wasn't about closing the church or bringing a white minister in. But he said "it would be a good idea to have the

meeting if nothing else, just to find out what they were thinking."
Even though it had been more than a month since my brother's
funeral I knew that with white people coming to talk about the
church they would be interested in what was going on.

I wanted to know anything that the white men were thinking,
minister or not. We set the place of the meeting at my house for the
following Saturday morning giving Gertrude enough time to cook
and it gave me enough time to think.

Beulah and my sisters arrived at daybreak. When the men arrived
from Rose Hill, William introduced them. The first was a rather
tall and elderly man whose name was Reverend Kentwood
Franklin from Bay Springs. The other two looked very similar to
each other. They were both about six feet tall, thin, and looked to
be about fifty years of age. One man's name was Newton Kemper
and the other was Dennis Kemper, from Rose Hill.

The first thing that I noticed about the men was quite obvious all
three of them were wearing white suits and each wore a black bow
tie. Reverend Franklin who was the Bishop of Jasper County began
by asking if we had chosen a minister, he said, "if you are still
looking I would like to recommend a boy from Jackson who I
believed would serve you colored people in as fine as manner as
Joseph had."

We were all dumbfounded. No one spoke for what seemed like an
eternity, when Harriet said "we don't need any white folks coming
in the name of the Lord treating us as if we cannot make decisions
for ourselves." She went on to say, "I don't mean no harm, but you
can get back on the same wagon that brought you here and go back
to wherever you came from." I looked toward the doorway, and to
my surprise, Gertrude was smiling and nodding her head in
agreement. They left without another word being spoken.

CHAPTER 14

HARD CHOICES

It just wasn't in Jasper County or even Mississippi that things seemed to be going amiss. In the middle of all of this turmoil, our government, the same government that stood by and did nothing about the virtual re-enslavement of colored people; were now asking these same people to all of sudden, forget what had happened, and sign up for the draft.

Even though we had no rights as men, our government wanted us to go thousands of miles across some sea, to fight and possibly die for the rights of other men, in some foreign country, when in fact we had no rights in our own country.

My brothers and I would often sit around and debate this issue; even a few times as we put out fires that the Klan had set. I remember how nervous Gertrude was about this whole thing, upon hearing that William and I may be drafted. By 1917, every able bodied colored man in Paulding was told that all eligible men had a patriotic duty to register for the draft; a boy one day and a man the next.

By this time, it was more than just a rumor that oil had been found in Jasper County. Colored people started losing their land, some in very strange and questionable ways; you would see a family one day, and the next day they were gone; or you would hear about some tragedy that had happened to them. It seemed as if there were two kinds of luck, both bad for colored folks, who were losing their property, and many time, their lives.

White folks, many who were share croppers, began to have unexpected good luck especially those who wore hoods, and would throw torches through colored folks windows at night.

Colored folks were being run off their land, or losing their lives. The white folks were taking their property, and the fruits thereof. It was about 1916, when Gertrude began talking about us going up North, she was concerned about the children, especially the three younger ones, Fred, Ruby and Flora who were growing up in the Ante Bellum South, with all of its horrors.

I told her that the Land of Lincoln and what it had promised really didn't exist anymore, if it ever had. It was about this time, that World War One was really at its peak, and the U. S. Army, was taking colored soldiers, and sending them to France.

The colored folks had mixed emotions about sending our boys off to war, and possibly never coming back. We were proud to fight for our country, but many, were tired of the country fighting us.

I remember my sister Hattie saying, "Why should we send our boys off to fight in a white man's war when a white man burned our house down last week? If anything, there is a war right here in Jasper County."

"I am not saying that we need to have a war with the white man, but it seems that the white man has a war with us, and to my recollect, always has. I don't want my boys going to war, I need them here, to help me rebuild."

Most colored people felt the same way. In fact there was a lot of hand wringing and grief over this issue, to the point that I thought it just might cause a big problem in our community. That is until early October of 1916, when my brother William called together what now would be considered a community meeting. It was held at the old Spring Hill Baptist Church.

As I said, William had attended college, and was a teacher at the Spring Hill School. He had educated many of the folks in and around Paulding and although he was colored, he was well respected and was held in high regard by colored and white people. He was one of the most educated and well spoken men that I have ever known, and it seemed as though when he spoke, even the birds stopped singing, to listen.

It was a Saturday afternoon, when everyone gathered at the church, there was so many folks that William decided to give his talk outside under the old brush arbor because there wasn't enough room in the church.

This was an important meeting and everyone wanted to attend. The site that was chosen was, bitter-sweet. It had been barely two years since my brother Joseph had been murdered, and the meeting was being held on the grounds where he started the Spring Hill church located next to the cemetery where Joseph was buried.

Our memories of him and the hurt just came flooding back. It was for this reason, that Gertrude and I felt it best for Beulah and her two children, Anna and Richard to ride with us. We thought that it would help her with the healing process. William and I believed that it was our responsibility to help raise Joseph and Beulah's children. In fact there wasn't a day that passed, that either Gertrude, I, or both of us, did not visit her home.

Anna and Richard were quite young when their father died and Beulah insisted that they not forget the memory of their father; that is why she pushed so hard for all of us to attend this meeting. And though at times she could seem quite distant, on this Saturday Beulah had all of her wits about her and was very focused and sharp.

I remember the Sheriff standing outside of his office (most likely wondering where all the colored's were going). It seemed as though he was going to stop someone to ask, that was until, he saw my wagon approach, and when his eyes met Beulah's gaze I saw all the questions and starch go out of him. He looked down at his shoes and would not raise his head. Beulah looked at him as though he was dirt, and raised her chin as we rode by. I looked back at him after we had gone past about eighty yards; he was still looking down and he quickly turned and walked back into his office and closed the door.

The atmosphere at the meeting looked as though it was a picnic; all the women brought food, and the children were running around playing. But all of the men had a very serious look of concern on their faces. My brother William walked over to me, Franklin and Tommie. We were all standing together talking about what it must have been like when our father use to hold meeting like this, and the gumption it had to have taken to do so.

William asked us if we thought that there would be such a crowd. I told him that we had no idea, but even the angels would come listen to what he had to say.

He gave a squeeze on my shoulder and with that sad smile of his he walked over to the steps of the church where he could be seen by everyone. I never will forget the words that he used to open his speech. "Brothers and Sisters, family, if you will, we come together today with concern; concern for our children, concern for ourselves, concern for our future and concern for our country."

He went on to talk about how our ancestors, our mothers and fathers who had helped build this great county; because it was on the backs of slaves that America had come so far, so fast, and even though colored people had faced so many injustices, they had overcome and grown even stronger.

He said that it was our duty to serve and furthermore, our duty to lead. That we owed it to our past to be involved in everything that America did. We built this country, we are part of this country and we may not see it now, but we will be part of the future of this county. And for this reason he felt that it was our duty to fight and possibly die for the defense of this country.

He continued by saying that "everyone in his family," that meant our family, "that was of draft eligible age, had already registered." I recall that it was so quiet I could hear the leaves rustling from the breeze. I remember at the end of his speech a cheer went up that had to have been heard all the way to Jackson.

I am sure that William's back was sore that night because everyone there slapped him on the back at least ten times and I myself at least, twenty five. I was so proud and yet so scared, scared for him. I knew that he would do great things, that is, if the white man would let him.

I thought about Joseph and my blood ran cold. But when I looked at William's sad smile as the people continued to congratulate him, I said to myself, how could anything that God created not love William too.

The meeting then, turned into an outing, and the outing turned into an event, that lasted, long, long, long, after dark. I believe every colored man of draft age, registered, it was my sister Harriet, who again said, that "she felt that it was wrong, we could fight and die for our county, but we couldn't even vote without taking a test and paying Poll Tax."

Name:	**Hiram R Cusis**
	[Hiram R Cruise]
	[Hiram R Cruise]
Age in 1910:	32
Estimated birth year:	abt 1878
Birthplace:	Mississippi
Relation to Head of House:	Head
Father's Birth Place:	Georgia
Mother's Birth Place:	United States of America
Spouse's name:	Gertrude Cusis
Home in 1910:	Beat 1, Jasper, Mississippi
Marital Status:	Married
Race:	Black
Gender:	Male
Neighbors:	View others on page

Household Members:	Name	Age
	Hiram R Cusis	32
	Gertrude Cusis	30
	William H Cusis	12
	Harriet E Cusis	11
	Joseph H Cusis	9
	Chester A Cusis	8
	James R Cusis	6
	Fred D Cusis	4
	Ruby Cusis	2
	Flora B Cusis	4/12

110

THE FAMILY CRUISE

Hiram Revels Cruise & Adalade Edwards-Cruse
Circa 1920

Hiram Revels Cruise

Fred Douglas Cruise

Letha Wolford-Cruise-Brown

Matthew Cruise with Mama Sarah Obama, Saiya, Kenya 2010

Matthew Cruise visits Kenya, 2010

Matthew Cruise, Bumala, Kenya 2010

CHAPTER 15

40TH COUSINS

Although everybody registered for the draft only three colored men were called. We sent them off in style. All of them returned, except one returned broken. It was one of the Hosey boys who served in one of the colored units that saw action in France.

Though many saw him as a hero he thought of himself as half a man. Maybe it was because his wife had actually called him half of a man the night she left him and moved to Jackson.

After Hosey's wife left, my brother William did everything in his power to make his life more comfortable. He went as far as to invite Hosey to live in his home. I think William felt that he was personally responsible for what had happened to him because he had encouraged us all to register for the service.

The young man did eventually move to William's house. I would stop by from time to time to see if I could help him in any way. On some days he would help me deliver meat.

The second Saturday of the month was always a big day for me. It was the day that I delivered all special orders to people in Paulding, chitterlings, hog maws, things that I had no way of keeping fresh in my smoke house. I spent most of the day delivering and selling meat but on this day I sold everything I had in the wagon. Financially it had been one of my best days.

I took my time cleaning my tools. I had several butcher's knives, an axe, two saws, and a carving knife. As I placed them in the compartment under the driver's seat my utensils shined in the setting sun. I was proud that I was able to make a good living for Gertrude and my family. As I climbed back into the wagon I looked up to see two young colored soldiers walking along the road. They looked as though they were carrying everything that they owned in the world. They seemed tired but happy. I asked them if they needed a ride. I didn't recognize them and realized that they were not from Paulding.

I stopped the wagon asked them where they were going and asked them if I could help. They told me their names, one said "I am Thomas Bogan" and the other said, "I am Kendell Warner. The first thing I noticed about Bogan was his smile, a smile that could shame the sun. It was broad and white which was in complete contrast to his midnight colored skin. He was dark as the night about six foot two and had the wide chest of a bull.

Warner in contrast was much smaller physically about five feet nine at best but as I looked closer his muscles were like ropes that wrapped tightly around his frame. He had the most interesting eyes they were brown with circles of blue and they danced from place to place as he was constantly surveying his surroundings. He was light skin like Gertrude he was what the white folks called a mulatto.

They were both very young and I would have been surprised if they were a day over twenty one. They both were from Georgia, where my father had been born. They said, "We have walked from Georgia, and through parts of Alabama, heading to New Orleans."

They went on to say "We on the way to New Orleans where we plan to work and finish learning French, and someday plan to return to Paris."

This chance encounter would literally forever change my life. I commented on how surprised I was that they had walked so far. I asked how long it had been since they first started. Warner shrugged his shoulders and said "Sir there is one thing that we are use to is walking." Bogan chimed in and said "Yes, we soldiers and can walk from here to Texas without breaking a sweat." Then

Warner added with a smile in his eyes, and said "that's right and back again too."

Although I was forty years old, I realized that I had lived a very sheltered life and I personally had never been out of Jasper County let alone, the State of Mississippi. Whereas these young men, boys really, had not only been outside of the United States but had taken a active role in defense of our country and not only helped shape the future of our country but also helped shape the future of the world.

They seemed to be wise beyond their years and I knew that they had seen things that I would never see. I'm not talking about war and killing, I was no stranger to violence and death. I couldn't count the times that I have washed blood from my hands or saw fear and death in someone's eyes, but I have never experienced life in the manner which these two had.

They went on to tell me about their time in the service of living in the trenches and how bullets and bombs exploded around them. How the sound and smell of death was constantly in their ears, and their noses. But it seemed even in a far off land they could not escape the sadness and the madness of the white man's hate and fury.

They told me of an incident when their units were forced to remove their gas mask and give them to men in a white unit. They were then ordered into battle where the Germans used mustard Gas on them. It brought tears to their eyes as they told the story of how so many of our good boys went down never to rise again. I couldn't help but think about the Hosey boy who was left half of what he once was.

I to felt the sting of tears in my eyes and just as the sun was setting and my anger continued to rise when one of the young soldiers asked me to stop for a moment. He took out his canteen and

117

removed the lid and took a long deep drink wiping his mouth he passed the canteen to my other new friend who did the same. He attempted to pass the canteen to me but I am not a drinking man so therefore I declined.

They both laughed and look at each other and said in one voice, "Mo' fore' me." Again, they started talking about New Orleans and the good times they hoped awaited them there.

They started in on telling me even though they had been to war they had seen remarkable things in a place called Paris, France. They said that, "In Paris no one cared if you were colored or not, that a man was a man, and a woman, a woman; and that is all they needed to know before they would get together; that France was a place where colored men really could be free."

I told them that we were free; that Mr. Lincoln had freed the slaves; they both started to laugh again shaking their head and said, "Cousin, you are not free like us."

Bogan continued by saying "you see in Paris, no one cared if you were with a white woman or not. No one cared if you walked on the same side of the street as they did and most of all no one cared if your skin was darker than theirs. No one there called you Boy, or Nigger. They called you a man or an American G.I."

As I sat trying to digest what they had said I could see torches burning in the wood about fifty feet off the road. I could hear what sounded like an angry conversation. As I slowed the wagon Bogan and Warner jumped off each side they pounced like cats and quickly disappeared into the woods moving quickly and deliberately, one went North and the other South.

I wasn't sure what they were doing but my attention was drawn away from them when I heard the cries of a woman.

I immediately climbed down from the wagon and placed a hand axe in the waistband of my trousers in the small of my back. I walked in the direction from where I heard the cries. What I saw made my blood run cold.

Two men had a young colored girl pinned to the ground and the third one was on the top of her. She couldn't have been any more than fourteen of fifteen years old not even as old as my daughter Harriet. Each man at her side had an arm and a leg in their hands they had her spread out and the man on top was having his way with her.

He cupped her mouth with his hands and yelled "Shut up you darkie, you know you like this you know you want this." There was another white man standing behind him who said "hurry up Pete it my turn again."

Just then, the girl must have bitten his hand because he yelled out in pain and then started to punch her in the face another white man appeared and kicked her in the side of the head.

The one they called Pete stood up with his pants still around his ankles and yelled over his shoulder "go head Lem you can have her I am about done with this black bitch, anyway. We done had her here for two days. Hell we all should be sore and there is not much left of her anyway."

As Lem pressed down on top of her I made out that the one that had kicked her in the head was the Deputy who had come to Joseph's house the day that he was murdered. He was the one that smiled and said, "We don't want no trouble out you people, ya'll hear." I remembered his smile because he had a mouth full of rotten teeth, probably from the tobacco that he chewed; just then he spit tobacco juice into the eyes of the girl. She cried out from the burn, they laughed and started passing the whiskey jug. What happened next is imprinted in my mind forever.

Everything was as if it was in slow motion; Bogan came from the right and then Warner from the left. They were upon the group of white men like panthers upon their prey. When Lem shouted get that boy I began to move in a straight line to confront him and as he walked toward me I could see his rotten teeth. He looked at me and said, "You the brother of that nigger that was killed at the dipping vat; now we are just going to have to kill you too."

It was quick it was violent it was bloody, it was efficient, Bogan and Kendell had both removed their shirts and each had a knife in the left hand with their right they cupped the mouth of the Deputy, and the man that stood directly beside him.

It looked as though in unison they both punched their knives into the back of their prey about the middle of their back. Again in unison they cut the throats of the two men.

Bogan nearly severed the head of one of them; they moved quickly to the two men directly in front of them they overpowered them as they stabbed them in the chest. The man who was waiting to get on top of the girl saw what was happening and tried to run.

He ran straight toward me. I then stepped out from behind the tree and sank my hand axe deep into his forehead. It was all over in less than two minutes. We had killed five white men; I fell to my knees I didn't know what to do first, to pray or to vomit. I did both.

When I finally looked up Bogan, Warner, and the girl were all looking down at me. I wiped my mouth and stood up as they helped me to my feet. Bogan retrieved his shirt and wrapped it around the girl. To my surprise she stood there like the oak tree that I had hid behind, solid and strong. In her eyes was the look for the ages. I then took a closer look at her and saw that she was a beautiful young woman. She was as black as coal and more beautiful than a diamond. I didn't recognize her family features and ask her where she was from and who was her family?

She told us that she was from Greenville and her name was Rachael Adams. She went on to say how she had been taken by the men who had stopped her on the road and forced her into the woods.

She told us that she wasn't sure how long it had been, but she thought that she had been held for the better part of two days. She said that they had done all kind of things to her and finally she began to cry. Then Kendell said, "don't cry, we be your family now."

I took her to the wagon and sat her next to the driver's seat. Thomas had already pulled the bodies deeper into the woods along the rushing creek which was pregnant from the snow melting from the nearby hills. Kendell asked "what are we going to do with the bodies, bury them, or burn them up?"

I told them that we would bury them here close to the bank of the creek because I know this area well and in a few weeks the creek will cover this area from here to over yonder as I pointed to my left. It will cover the bank for about forty to sixty yards. There would not be any sign that anything was ever buried.

Thomas said, "Let's get busy." They both returned to the wagon and took out short handle shovels they had in their back packs. I removed my shovel from the wagon it was a long handle shovel for which I usually used to shovel manure and I thought to myself that's what I was doing now burying manure.

Kendell said, "Wait I need a drink," and I replied at this point I could use one too. Bogan looked at me and said "My man." He went to the wagon and retrieved the bottle that was three times the size of the canteen. He removed the cork and wiped the top with his sleeve and gave me the bottle.

I am not a drinking man and the smell made my eyes water and my nose run. As I took my first drink I immediately began to cough but my weak and shaking legs did come back to me. Although I was use to blood I had never killed a man before and to tell you truth, I cannot describe the feeling that was going through me at that moment.

It wasn't that I was regretting what I had done I felt self assured about that but my body seemed as if it was every place at the same time. The drink brought me back together.

It was then I realized that Rachael was standing beside me. As I continued to cough she took the jug from my hand and took a long hard swallow herself. She started to cough as well. This brought Bogan's smile into full bloom. In a very soft voice Rachael tried to thank us for what we had done.

But Bogan cut her off and said, "This was our duty and after all our lives was in danger too." Rachael had a puzzled look on her face and I to wondered what he meant; as if he was reading our minds he went on to explain his statement.

He said, "If we had not taken action it would have cost us our lives, our lives as men. You see a real man colored or white would not have done what they did to this beautiful young child, and had we just gone on by as if nothing was happening we could never again look at our faces in a mirror."

"And another thing, a colored man can't call himself a man if he had allowed them to do it and act as though nothing was happening. We were not able to prevent it but we definitely did something about it. I am not saying that we made it right. I am not saying we made it go away. I am just saying a man cannot stand by and do nothing." Kendell said, "Man! You and your speeches let's move."

Even though she was a child you could see in her face a look of understanding. At that moment I think she and I grew and got a better understanding about life.

I climbed into the wagon and pulled it out of sight. We then began to dig the graves and as we were digging Bogan's words keep echoing in my head. I couldn't shake what he had said; he was right, had we not taken some action I would have felt less than a man the same as I felt when I sat with my brother's body the night after his murder. I didn't take any action after my brother Joseph was killed.

Although it was a full moon as we were digging Rachael stood in the mist of us holding the lantern so that we would have enough light for what we needed to do. Bogan sang softly as we worked and had anyone not known what we were doing it would have seemed that we were having a pleasant time.

After about an hour Rachael began to cry again. It was no wonder after what she had been through and what she was witnessing now. I stopped and asked her if she was alright which really in my mind, was a silly question. Who could be alright after going through what she has experienced.

She said, "Yes, I was just thinking about what Mr. Bogan said and I believe what he talked about how that must have been the thought on my daddy's mind when he left us. It was about five years ago when I was only eight my father couldn't stop some white men from raping my mother and my two older sisters. Afterwards, he was never the same. It wasn't from the beating that he took it was because they made him watch them rape his family. He never felt that he was a man again. He thought that he couldn't do anything about it." Bogan, Kendell, and I, stood there silently and the only sound we could hear was Rachael's soft sobs and the rushing water of the creek that somehow seemed to honor this sacred moment as it hushed the sound of the currents.

It was Kendell who broke the silence by speaking actually a little too loud not quite yelling but definitely far above a normal voice as he tried to regain his composure. What he said next, I will never forget. "We ain't no niggers." "We ain't no boys, we ain't no slaves; we don't bow down to no white man; or call him master, or even sir. We look them in the eyes, we don't move to the side to let them pass first and we will let them know that our women are just as good as theirs, and better."

Kendell went on to say, "When we were in France, I learnt me some history, not that stuff they taught us here, but real history. Our people come from Kings we haven't always been slaves. We the ones that built this county we have nothing to be ashamed of, if anything it is them the white folks who should be ashamed."

"They should be ashamed of the lies they told, and the things they have done, they should be ashamed of who they are and what they have become. Not all of them mind you, but a good many, to many! They know that in most things we do, we better than them."

"Bogan, we both know that all white people are not bad. We have both had some pretty good white people come into our lives. My grandfather was a good white man. You remember the white medic from Georgia who more than one time risked his life under fire to help colored soldiers. He carried some of them over his shoulder while bullets were whistling over his head." Bogan said, "Yes I remember and you're right there are some good white men I just don't know many of them." I thought back about the stories my father had told us about Lennon Ellis and if there ever was a good white man he surely was one but I would not get that pass Harriet.

It took us several more hours to finish the graves and everyone was bone tired but I had some concern about Rachael and figured she would need some female attention. I thought it best that I get her home where Gertrude could look after her and I could make some medicine so she could feel better. We washed the dirt from the shovels in the creek and made sure that there was no sign of what we had done. We cleaned up as best we could and started home.

It was well passed daybreak when we arrived and I could see Gertrude standing in the road. She started running toward our wagon as soon as she saw us coming. I jumped down from the wagon before the horses stopped as she ran into my arms.

She asked where I had been and I told her that we had not slept all night. She said that she knew something must be wrong because we had not spent a night apart, since the day we were married. She took her eyes off of me and looked up into the wagon and when saw Rachael she held her arms out and said "Come here baby."

I didn't have to say anything about it at that moment. It was as if she knew something bad had happened. Kendell and Bogan climbed from the wagon and gently helped Rachael down. Rachael hugged Gertrude's neck as if she was her own mother.

As they started for the house the three of us took the wagon into the barn. We unhitched the team and I went to the back of the barn to make some medicine for Rachael's wounds and something to help her rest. Henry and Joel came into the barn excited and asked what was going on? They saw Kendell and Bogan and stopped in their tracks. Joel asked if there was anything that they could do. Henry walked over to me and in a low voice asked, who are they?

Kendell walked over to Joel and introduced himself and Bogan. I told my boys to take them into the house and make them comfortable. When I finally entered the house I heard Henry and Joel asking them about the war. I told them that there will be plenty of time to talk later. What these men need right now is some sleep and so do I.

Gertrude had taken Rachael into our bed room and helped her wash herself and she gave her a dress. I knocked and gave the medicine to Gertrude and went back to join the others. Although it was early morning I told them we should all get some rest and that we would talk about our plans later.

It was early evening when I smelled the familiar aroma of Gertrude's cooking. It awakened me and to my surprise I was the last one to enter the kitchen. Bogan and Kendell were already eating and were stuffing themselves with fried chicken and mashed potatoes. We always had lemonade with every meal and on this day a fresh apple cobbler.

Rachael appeared to have recovered somewhat, but I wondered about her mind. After we finished eating we all went into the waiting room and Kendell said "what are we to do next?" We looked at each other and I realized that we had to make some decisions, careful decisions, decisions that we would live and possibly die by.

Gertrude said that Rachael had told her everything that had happened to her over the past two days. Gertrude didn't seem surprised that we had taken the action that we did and had a certain glow of approval in her eyes as she said, "I am very proud of all of you." I felt ten feet tall!

She looked at me and said, "Hiram I love you very much." It was the first time she had ever said those words in front of strangers. But as I now think about it Bogan, Kendell and Racheal were now family; she went on to say "Whatever happen, happens. I am with you to the end." All I could do is nod my head and before I could speak Bogan started in by saying to Gertrude, "I been in the war and I have seen many brave men and Ma'am you and your husband is right up there with the best."

We talked well into the night and by this time William came in. I was glad that he was there. He seemed to always be there for me when I needed him the most. He was always the voice of reason.

We told him about the events of yesterday and all he said was, "I am glad you were there for her and that none of you got hurt. I was surprised at his comment but I said nothing in response. Kendell said, "thank you sir." William asked Gertrude how Rachael was doing and he wanted to meet this brave young girl. We considered all options and decided that Rachel would remain with Gertrude and me, but Bogan and Kendell felt it best to continue their journey.

I told them that there would be no rush and they were welcome to stay as long as they wanted to but Kendell said, "We think it is best that we move on in the morning." Bogan nodded his head in agreement and asked Gertrude if he could have another piece of pie. She smiled widely and said "I am way ahead of you I made one for each of you." We all laughed.

Early the following morning before day break, I saddled two horses and told Bogan and Kendell that I thought it was best that they rode the rest of the way. If there was any trouble coming, I wanted these two fine young men to be as far away as possible. We were all standing along the road that led away from Paulding and Kendell said as they rode slowly down the side of the hill. "After all, we be 40th cousins, at least." That made me feel good I nodded my head and said to Gertrude at last I understand.

1870 United States Federal Census

Name:	**Janes Crase** *[James Cruise]*
Birth Year:	abt 1836
Age in 1870:	34
Birthplace:	Georgia
Home in 1870:	Center Beat, Jasper, Mississippi
Race:	Black
Gender:	Male
Value of real estate:	View image
Post Office:	Paulding

Household Members: Name	Age
Janes Crase	34
Hanah Crase	37
Mary Crase	20
Caroline Crase	15
Barbary Crase	13
Ellen Crase	11
Alice Crase	8
Amanda Crase	6
William C Crase	4
Hurit E Crase	2
Ann E Crase	7/12
Rich Ferguson	27

CHAPTER 16

OUR NEW DAUGHTER

Rachael continued to live with us and we watched her blossom into a lovely young woman. We raised her as one of our own. She was very beautiful, and smart as a whip. She loved school, she loved life, and what made us proudest of all she loved God.

She was always the first in the wagon on Sunday morning eager to get to the Spring Hill Baptist Church. She sang in the choir and after two years she taught the young folks in our Sunday School Class.

Yes, Rachael had become quite the young lady. Gertrude and I were happy to see that she had put that horrible night behind her. The only reminder from that horrible night was a scar where she was kicked, but she covered it with her long wavy hair.

As I said, Rachael was quite the student, and Gertrude and I decided to send her to college. She was the first girl in our family to do so. We thought that she would go to school in Mississippi, but she surprised us and said that she wanted to attend school in New Orleans.

We did not have a problem with her decision but we knew that it would take more money. We had enough money to pay for school in Mississippi because of the land grant scholarships but after I talked with Gertrude we decided that we wanted her to attend the college she desired to attend.

That night when we went to bed Gertrude told me that Rachael and Kendell had been writing letters to each other for over a year. It seemed that Bogan and Kendell had never made it to Paris. They choose to seek their fortune in New Orleans instead. I often wondered what had become of them and now at last I knew that they were safe and sound.

Every six months or so, the whole Cruise clan would have a big get together. It started right after Joseph was murdered. It was a way of saying without saying in words how much we loved one another. It was a way of saying how much we cared for each other and how much we valued each and every member of our family; like a tree values the seed that it comes from and the branches that it produces. We value every branch on our family tree.

We would talk about the past, we would talk about the present, and we would talk about our dreams and the future. We looked at our children with pride and the younger ones would look at us with awe, especially when we would tell stories about their grandpa and grandma.

We told them about how grandpa was bought by Mr. Ellis from a slave owner in the Blue Ridge Mountains of Georgia; how he was brought to Jasper County when he was just a young boy. And how he later met and married our mother Hannah. How proud he was that he earned money while he was a slave. How he was so proud of the fact that he learned to read and write long before he was set free.

Our children loved to hear the history of our family and colored people in general, and we loved to tell it. I often wondered just what it was that our ancestors held on to because they never lost hope. Hope for freedom, hope for family and hope for someone to lead them from the bondage of slavery.

Was it the excitement in the stories or was it the lessons that the children learned about their ancestors or was it simply just feeling that they were a part of a people who sought the promise land? For me it was both learning about our ancestors and knowing that I belonged to someone special, our family.

William and I never missed the chance to take the boys out into the woods beyond the creek. It was our chance to talk and to teach. It was also our chance to learn just what type of young men these boys were becoming.

We often spent hours just talking and teaching them the art of selecting proper roots and herbs that grew on the creek bank. I told the boys that selecting the proper herbs was very much like selecting the proper wife.

You see, it took a very special herb to make the right medicine for what ails you. Just choosing any herb wouldn't do, and if you chose the wrong herb it would make you sick or worse. My advice about choosing a wife is to choose but choose carefully. Like I said, just like you have to choose the right herb you have to choose the right wife. When my son Chester asked me how will he know when he has the right woman? I told him that he would just know.

When I would say things like this to the boys William would laugh but would always agree. All of us raised our children the same way. We didn't give out advice about life if we hadn't lived it.

We taught our boys to always take care of their wives and never to beat them or talk harshly to them. It was what our father taught us, and it was the way we treated our wives.

I knew that I was blessed because there was only one choice for me and I knew from the beginning that she would be my herb. She has always made me well every time I saw her face. If I could ever give our sons a blessing it would be that these fine young boys would find an everlasting love the same kind that God had given me.

The women had their hands full because there were twice as many girls as there were boys. They did the things that women do as far as teaching them to cook and take care of a family. But one day we just happened to catch them in one of their special training sessions.

As usual it was Harriet who was holding court. By this time she and Gertrude were seeing things more eye to eye and as they were standing side by side as they were giving a lecture on how to control your husband. We didn't want to disturb the conversation so we quietly slipped to the side keeping ourselves hidden behind some trees.

We could hear every word but we were careful to keep ourselves out of view. From what we were hearing we had no problem keeping everybody in our party quiet, especially the older boys. I think all of our mouths were hanging open as we continued to listen to Harriet telling the girls how they would have to establish as early as possible, even before marriage, who was really in control.

Harriet sounded like a Baptist preacher as she told the girls, "Girls remember there is a fine art for what I am about to tell you. You have to let the man think that he is the one who is in charge; you see, he needs to feel like he is the one running the house."

To my complete surprise Gertrude chimed in by saying "in most ways he does." Harriet scoffed and said "yea, but not in the most important ways. You see let me tell you about men; a man is good for everything and at the same good for nothing." She went on to say "the trick is not teaching them what to think but how you want them to think."

"Once you teach them how to think then they will only think about the things you want them to think. You have to make them think that what they are thinking is their idea; it's not; it's what you want them to think. This is not something that is easy to learn and it won't come overnight it takes practice and work. Believe me once you get it down it will give you every benefit of marriage and it will make your life, both of ya'll really, so much better."

"You see a man doesn't know what he really wants other than wanting you. So, you have to teach him what he wants and how to get what he wants, and oh yes, how to get you too. Girls it's us that do the choosing we just have to make them think that they choose us first; as I said there is an art to the whole thing."

All I could hear from our crowd was giggles and laughs; I turned to look at William and I swear he was giggling too which made me laugh. My sister Anna looked up and pointed toward us and said "here are the men folks."

I looked at Gertrude with searching eyes wondering if her mother or aunt had given her the same instructions. Gertrude knew that we may have heard some of what they were telling the girls. She blushed but Harriet just scoffed and waived her hands in the air and said "ya'll remember what I just told you."

During all of the time of the "chicken chatter," the women had prepared quite a feast. For the first time Rachael cooked the main meal of fried chicken, hot water cornbread, collard greens with ham hocks and my favorite fried sweet potatoes topped off with butter and sweet Louisiana sugar on the top.

The women really outdid themselves because it was a special dinner in honor of our late brother Joseph. We always sat a place for him in his honor and his memory.

There were pitchers of ice tea, lemon aid, and cool butter milk so everyone's favorite drink was before them. As we ate I just couldn't help but bring up the conversation that we had just heard between Harriet and the girls. Maybe I was pushed by the look on my son's faces, Chester, Fred, Walter, and Daniel. Maybe it was the smug look from Harriet, who by the way had never been married a day in her life, but she knew everyone who was, and was quick to give advice. Whatever it was I just had to say it so I asked Gertrude, "Honey, what were you all really talking about?"

As usual Harriet tried to butt in but William shushed her to silence and said "I want to hear this." My boys in unison said "yes we want to hear it too mama." Again all the girls started to giggle; that is, all but Harriet, but true to herself she always did what William asked of her so she kept silent. Gertrude said "it was nothing, just girl talk."

I saw right then that I wouldn't get any serious conversation from her but decided to leave one last comment; I said, "these are some of the reasons that black men don't get the respect from women that they should." It was as if the skies had opened and balls of hell fire were falling from the heavens. All at once everyone grabbed their plates and went in different direction, all except Gertrude and I who sat facing each other.

At that moment I wish I hadn't said what I did but it was too late, it was said. As Harriet walked pass Gertrude, I heard her say "get him honey and don't hold back."

I asked "what does that mean?" As I watched Harriet walk away, I looked back at my wife who had sat back in her chair and crossed her legs tightly, so much so that I thought she would pull the hem from the dress that rested on top of her beautiful legs. I knew these signs from the many years that we had been married which accompanied her stern look.

I knew I was about to be talked to very deeply. She studied my face for a moment with her blue green eyes and to my surprise she began to smile. I lost the battle and the war all at the same time and she didn't have to say a word. I said never mind I understand and she said yes, I knew that you would. I asked for another piece of pie.

William returned with a flush face because he laughed so hard he made the sun go down. I heard Freddie say "what just happened here?" I turned and said to him "son right now you just wouldn't understand" and I thought to myself, I am not sure I do either.

Even though we made ends meet with something to spare, it wasn't the best of times for Jasper County. We decided to borrow five hundred dollars from M. H. Turner and Sons, who later sold our loan to S. D. Russell; we finally paid it off seven years later. School started one week after Easter. We went to church knowing that it would be some time before we were all together again.

It was a beautiful Sunday in March, the flowers were in early bloom and the weather was warm for that time of year. Beside Gertrude, Rachael was the prettiest woman in the church. Gertrude was dressed in pink, and Rachael in yellow, Gertrude wore a bonnet and Rachael had spring blossoms in her hair. She was so excited it was not just that she was going away to college but she was going to sing a solo at church service.

It had been all she talked about for at least a week. The song that she selected was "His Eyes are On the Sparrow." Rachael was as beautiful as an angel and her voice brought us all to tears. It wasn't a dry eye in the whole church and it was as though she was telling all of us that she was going to be alright.

Compared to the day that I first saw her she was as different as night and day. She was strong with more determination and with renewed strength we knew that she would be alright.

My brother William and his wife Anna gave her a wonderful send off party. It was quite the event because Rachael was the first woman to attend college from our family and as you know we Cruises' do things big.

She left for college the next week but she returned home every summer and taught the summer session to her bible class. She graduated four years later with a state certified teaching certificate. We knew that our daughter was an exceptional young woman. She majored in French and it wasn't a surprise to any of us when she took a job in New Orleans, and one year later she became Mrs. Rachael Adams Cruise Warner.

I gave her away and Bogan was the best man and as I said we Cruises' do things big. She wore Gertrude's wedding dress and the wedding was held on the same spot where Gertrude and I were married. It was one of the happiest days of our lives. They produced three grand children and each one of them speaks French like a Frenchman. After Kendell became a successful textile trader he moved his family to Paris. The last time we heard from them was 1935 the year that Gertrude died. Dreams do sometime come true.

CHAPTER 17

THE FINAL STRAW

By 1925, my sons William Henry, Joel and John had moved out and started a family of their own. Henry and his wife Ethel Nicholson were the first ones to move north to the Land of Lincoln. He was soon followed by my Nephew, Isaac (Ike) Cruise. A few years prior to his leaving Henry married Ethel. John and Joel were both married within a year of each other. John moved to Georgia and Joel to Arkansas where they both followed my profession and became farmers and butchers.

Like my father and mother, Gertrude and I loved each other very much. A testament to our love was the fact that we had a total of seventeen children and raised them to be productive citizens. Another reason with the exception of the night when I first brought Rachael home, we never spent a full day apart during the thirty two years we were married. We enjoyed each other as friends, lovers and bearers of the same spirit.

Life continued to have its ups and its downs. After all we were still living in the state of Mississippi. Colored people had come a long way, some may say to long but I felt we hadn't come far enough.

My brother William had become one of the most popular colored people in Jasper County and he had one of the best minds I have ever known, and by far the biggest heart. There wasn't a person white or colored who didn't know who he was and at the time, I wasn't sure if this was good or bad. Even though he was loved by many there were those who hated him. He had enough enemies to cause all of us some concern.

However, my brother being the man that he was, and having the father we had, like our father he never showed any fear. He always told it like it was. He was the same with everyone including me. William was always positive. He saw the good in everything and everybody and his positive frame of mind rubbed off on everyone around him. Most people in Paulding loved him for what he was, a great man not just a great colored man.

Christmas of 1924, we held our Christmas festivities at my house. For as long as I could remember the Cruise family all gathered at one of our houses for a Christmas meal and the giving of presents. When Joseph was alive he would always give the Christmas prayer. But for the last eleven years William offered the prayer.

All of my brothers and sisters and their families were there, Barbari, Ellen, Amanda, Harriet, Anna, William and me. It was more than enough people to fill up the two large rooms at the front of the house.

I can't remember everything that William prayed about but he thanked God for his family, for his wife, and for all that God had given to him. He thanked God that he was blessed to be the first "free born male" in the family and for giving us our wonderful parents, who in spite of being born slaves, prayed and hoped for the day that we would all be free.

The last thing that he said sent chills down my spine. He thanked God for the number of years that he allowed him to be on this earth and prayed that I would take up the mantle if something would happen to him.

There was more than enough food to feed everyone, more than twice. Before the fun got to far carried away, William said that he had something to talk to us about.

Before he could get into what he wanted to say, Harriet cut him off; as I said before, she fancied herself quite the talker and had a way of taking over conversations. She had done so for years, it was just her way.

I really hadn't paid too much attention to her because I was more concerned about Gertrude. The holidays usually brought the best out in her, but I had noticed that today she seemed to be a little distant and maybe upset.

I was just about to ask her if she was okay, when she did something that I had only seen her do maybe three times in her life. You see my wife is the most polite person that I knew; she never raised her voice or had a harsh word for anyone. But on this occasion she let Harriet have it with "both barrels." It was a shock and surprise to everyone but what she said was true.

Gertrude just cut right in and told Harriet, maybe the reason you cut people off is because you feel you don't have much time left, it is disrespectful. It shows disregard for the speaker. What it says is I don't care what you are saying and I openly disrespect what you are thinking. I show my disregard for you by talking over you. All that counts is my point. I will not allow you to express your thoughts!

Harriet sat there with a look of shock and disbelief on her face. Everyone else could do nothing but smile. I believed that my smile was the widest until I looked at William. He didn't have a smile on his face he had a grin from ear to ear. Gertrude turned to William and said, "Continue with what you were saying please."

William announced that he was going to help the older colored people and for that matter anyone else who could not read. He said that starting next week he was going to start delivering the U.S. Mail; and to those who could not read he was going to stay and read their letters to them. He also said that if they would allow him he would try to help teach them to read. My sister Anna said "that is a wonderful, wonderful idea."

Colored folks had started moving north and would send money home but because most people in Paulding could not read or write they were unable to know whether they had received the money and how their family was doing. After everybody left Gertrude asked if I understood what William said in his prayer about "anything happening to him?" I told her that I would ask him the next day.

Later that night after everyone had gone home and we had cleaned up the house from another happy time spent with our family, Gertrude and I sat down on the couch holding hands as we did every night before we went to bed. She looked at me with such a serious look on her face I asked if there was something wrong.

I noticed her eyes started to tear and she said "I am sorry for telling your sister Harriet off but I just couldn't take it anymore." I started to say that it was alright because people, especially family should be able to say what is on their minds. She held my hand and told me that she was sick and felt that she was going to die. I felt that I had been kicked in the stomach by a mule.

She told me that she felt her sickness deep inside of her. She vowed that her sickness would be the only thing that would ever separate us. I didn't know what to say but I knew that I had to stop this from being so. I had a million questions going through my mind; what was she talking about how did she know and how could this happen? I knew that I could prevent it by making some medicine; there had to be a way. I knew that if Gertrude died, I would never be the same again. After all she was my reason for living.

For the next several months my main goal was to find a way to make my wife feel better; but little by little, maybe a month at a time, I could see her began to weaken. I tried every herb and potion that my father had taught me but nothing seemed to help for long. After a year my only hope was to try and help her maintain a

reasonable life. Sometimes I felt as though I was grasping at
straws. William and I tried every mixture of herbs that we could
think of; Gertrude seemed to improve but was still very sick.

William's influence had grown all over Jasper County. He had
become very popular every place he went people wanted his
opinion on some matter. He told me that the postmaster died, and
he was going to take the test to replace him. If he was selected he
would be the first colored postmaster in Mississippi.

He felt that he knew the job and could perform the task of being
Postmaster. The only question was would the white people in the
county allow him to do so. He said that in spite of the possible
outcome he was going to take the test. He said that they had
already tried to recruit someone from Laurel, Hattiesburg, and
Magee, but he still thought that he was the best man for the job.

By late March of 1926, it had become pretty much a certainty that
my brother, William Cruise would become the next postmaster of
Jasper County, Mississippi. Once again everybody was slapping
him on his back and every other Cruise that they could find.
Colored folks all around felt good when they heard the news; it
was as if William was uplifting us all. This news brought a smile
on Gertrude's face, a smile that I had not seen in sometime.

I remember being quite sad during these times, one because of
Gertrude, and two, because of a certain fear that I had concerning
William. I didn't know why at the time but it was a feeling that I
just couldn't shake. It seemed that I always felt a cold wind
blowing.

Even though it was 1926, and slavery had been over for more than
sixty years in many ways nothing had changed in Mississippi. The

white man felt that he still owned colored people and to them we were nothing more than property.

They didn't want us to vote they didn't want us to own land, they didn't want us to make our own money, and many of them didn't want us to even look them in the eye. The Klan was very much alive and active in Jasper County and throughout the entire South. They had visited William's house at least four times in the past week.

They had even burned a cross on my place a time or two in the last few weeks. We were all on edge but not afraid and all of my sons were excellent shots. Everyone knew that my son Freddie was among the best in the county. I believe that this is one of the reasons that the Klan didn't come around our house more often. I am sure that they knew in the end that they would win but being the cowards that they were, they chose the easy fights. Coming to my house would be no easy fight.

William came by the house as he often did when he had something troubling on his mind. He told me if something happened to him not that he thought it would, but if it did to make sure that his wife and children would leave Mississippi. He said that Anna had people in California and that is where he wanted them to go if he wasn't around to take care of them himself.

I asked him what he was talking about if he wasn't around, he smiled at me and shook his head and said, "Let me finish, Harriet," and we both started to laugh.

He went on to say how he thought a new world was coming; a world where colored and whites would treat each other as equals; no more sir and boy, just people being people. He said that it would not be the world that we live in today and we may not live to see it but he was sure that it was coming and the sooner the better. He hugged me and almost squeezed the breath out of me.

He gave me a stern look and said, "Take care of yourself and your family." As Gertrude entered the room he quickly left out the side door and went toward home. I never saw him alive again.

The next morning April 29, 1926, a white man shot and killed my brother William as he was going to work as the new postmaster of Jasper County. They killed him as he was going to do what he always did help people no matter who they were. Colored, whites or some who were undeserving; you see to William Charles Cruise it didn't matter who you were or what you were all that mattered was that you were a child of God and by God, he was going to do the best for you that he could.

William Charles Cruise was buried on May 7, 1926, at the Spring Hill Cemetery on the grounds of the Spring Hill Baptist Church founded by his brother Joseph. It was located about two miles from Paulding. He was buried beside Joseph who was also assassinated by a white man; neither one of them were ever brought to justice. They were both laid to rest alongside our parents.

That was it for me, I was done; I had grown tired of the secrets, I had grown tired of the white man's truths, I had grown tired of the sins, and the stains that would not wash away. I had grown tired of Jasper County, Mississippi I had grown tired of Mississippi. I decided to move because this was the last straw.

It took me a year to finally pay off the balance of the loan that we made the year that Rachael left for college. By this time the white people were using new ways of stealing our lands. Even though colored people paid off their loans many of them could not read and signed papers that gave the land to the white people.

Gertrude and I made sure that our debt was cancelled and we recorded the information at the court house before we left Mississippi.

1920 United States Federal Census

Name:	**Sy Lie** **[Sy Lee]**
Home in 1920:	**Southeast, Jasper, Mississippi**
Age:	**51**
Estimated birth year:	**abt 1869**
Birthplace:	**Mississippi**
Relation to Head of House:	**Father**
Father's Birth Place:	**Mississippi**
Mother's Birth Place:	**Mississippi**
Marital Status:	**Married**
Race:	**Black**
Sex:	**Male**
Able to read:	**Yes**
Able to Write:	**Yes**
Neighbors:	View others on page

Household Members: Name	Age
Anderson Lie	26
Malvina Lie	26
Edgar Lie	7
Ellen Lie	4
Anderson Lie	1
Sy Lie	51

PART THREE

CHAPTER 18

HUMAN TRAGEDY

My name is Matthew Cruise. I am now seventy five years old; I have finally found the answers that I have searched for since I was nine years old. I have spent most of my life in the service of people and the service to my country. I have healed enough to tell this part of my family's rich and proud history.

Tragedy hit our family in 1943, when my closest brother James, who I revered as a man among boys, accidentally shot and killed my cousin Pearlie Mae Cruise, who was my Uncle Walter's daughter. Pearlie Mae was a beautiful girl, she had long beautiful hair and her skin was the color of bronze. Her big brown eyes almost hypnotized you.

I can never forget the horror and disbelief on my cousin's face and the fear and terror that gripped me as she crumbled off the bed to the floor from the force of the bullet. Blood was everywhere, on the wall, the bed, and all over me. I was less than five feet from her, even though it was she that was shot, I was in shock and looked as if I had been shot also. To my utter dismay, for a second, I thought that James was going to kill himself. He was in shock and total disbelief. What he said next still haunts me to this very day.

He looked at me and said in an almost to calm a voice, "I won't live another year." In fact he died less than nine months later, as result of stepping on a nail and the negligence of Doctor Eubanks to give him a simple Tetanus shot. How ironic it was that his death certificate listed the cause of death as lock jaw. It was a description that in many ways rang true. I can't recall that this previously talkative outgoing boy saying more than five hundred words after that tragic day, the day that he predicted his own death.

I know that James always blamed himself for what happened, but it was an accident. We were playing cowboys and Indians when James took our father's shot gun from the closet. He used the gun instead of the broom stick that he used when we played outside. He pointed it back and forth at my cousin and then at me and said, "bang, bang, you're dead." Pearlie Mae and I laughed and ran around the room hiding on the other side of the bed while shooting back at him with our imaginary guns.

It was an accident. I am sure of this because James loved Pearlie Mae as much as everyone did. I know he had no malice in his heart for anyone and would have easily laid down his own life for both she, and I. Although he pulled the trigger, I know that it was an accident. I wish that I had her picture because I have tried to wipe from my mind the memory of that horrible day. Although I remember the funeral, I remember the casket, but I still can't clearly remember the events of that day.

Everyone in the family was in shock and dismay; but my brother James took it the hardest. After all he was just ten years old. He suffered the magnitude of what he had done much like a man three times his age.

What I am saying is he understood the magnitude of the accident he had caused and as a result it simply broke his spirit and in my mind it was a big part why he thought that he wouldn't live to become an adult. In a strange way I felt that he wanted to give his life as payment for what he took responsibility for.

It was during this tragic time that the issue of color was the issue in which my mother and my aunt Ceola, Pearlie Mae's mother, were able to bond. They were often ridiculed by their lighter skinned sister-in-laws because of their dark skin. They were looked down upon but they turned a perceived negative into a positive. To them being dark gave them a sense of pride. It was a symbol that they both wore as a badge of beauty. It was almost as though they had their own personal kinship.

After the death of Pearlie Mae their bond only grew closer. There was never any finger pointing, distribution of guilt or statements of responsibility; they mourned together until the day that aunt Ceola died.

My mother already had a burden to just feed her eight children. This unfortunate accident just added to that burden, but it did not break her. We never saw any signs of outward dismay. There was never a question that my mother was a very strong woman and now she was proving it.

In June of 1947, I remember that my whole family came together to celebrate the return of my uncle Hiram from the Civilian Conservation Camp (CCC), and to remember Abraham Lincoln and his Emancipation of Slavery. World War II was over and it was a happy time.

Food was being cooked by the ladies and the men were cooking ribs and goats on the pit. I remember that the men were talking among themselves, but they did not really include us children. I had no idea what the Emancipation of Slavery really meant or why they were celebrating this day. What did peak my interest was when I overheard them talking about life in Mississippi. They talked for hours. As the food was being prepared, my uncle Henry had much to say. He seldom came around because he was what we called back in those days "passing" himself off as a white man. However, he was well respected by the family simply because he was the oldest boy.

As he continued to talk I noticed that there was some emotion because they started to take issue with some of the things that

Uncle Henry said. I wanted to come closer and I did somewhat, but not within ear shot. I could barely make out that they were discussing the emotional subject of the difference between light and dark skinned people. This subject is still talked about even today. Many light skinned people still feel superior to people who have darker skin.

I have heard it said that in the city of Atlanta they would never have a dark skinned mayor. This mentality is divisive and I believe that it is the residue of self hate. As I said in my family I feel it ironic, that it was my aunts who had the problem with the darker skin of my mother and my aunt Ceola, but the men never seemed to have an issue, and until then, had never talked about it.

The way I see it, most men see beauty for beauty whether it be dark or light, and some women see beauty as a point of contention and make issue of the hue of one's skin. Yet it is difficult for most black women to see a black man marry a white woman. They often end their diatribe with the statements "you don't see many white men marrying black women, unless they are rich and famous, and beautiful; yet black men don't care how they look, as long as they are white."

I believe that the reason for contention between my family and my uncle Henry was quite simply that by him being lighter skin, he was ashamed of the family. By his actions, it was the family that was ashamed of him. We were, and are a proud family. There is no area or need for a member of the Cruise's to feel that they have to "pass." What we do is that we pass on to each other our zest for life, and our ability to take what we have and make the best out of any situation we may be in.

CHAPTER 19

THE TORCH IS PASSED

As my grandfather Hiram use to say "everybody comes from somebody, and from somewhere."

Charlie Cruise, whose mother was born in Africa about 1790, was born in the Blue Ridge Mountains of Georgia; about 1810, the father of James Cruise, born in the Blue Ridge Mountains of Georgia about 1834, the father of Hiram Revels Cruise, born in Jasper County, Mississippi on January 3, 1877, the father Fred Douglas Cruise, born in Jasper County, Mississippi on July 11, 1907, the father of Matthew Cruise, born in East Saint Louis, Illinois on May 1, 1935, the father of Matthew Jonathan Cruise, born in East Saint Louis, Illinois on November 10, 1957. These are the names of men who are the male descendants of a woman who was born in Africa.

My name is Matthew Cruise but as long as I can remember everybody called me "Boone." I am the fourth son of Fred Douglas Cruise and Letha Ora-Wofford-Cruise Brown. My father met my mother while she was a student at Lincoln University at Jefferson City, Missouri. After a whirlwind courtship they got married and moved to East Saint Louis in 1929, the year that the stock market crashed.

My parents continued the old Cruise saying "the Cruise family did everything in a big way." Together my parents had a total of eleven children, Floyd, Fred, James, Matthew, Leonard, Howard Leon, Haywood, Hiram Grady, twins who were still born, and my only sister, Wilma Freda Cruise Ray. Fred, James, Leonard, Haywood, and the twins have all passed away; the rest are still alive and kicking, but none higher than me. I am very proud of my family and I love each and every one of them very, very much. As you have seen the Cruise family has a rich and powerful history. It is my privilege and my honor not only to be a Cruise but to have the honor to continue telling my family's story.

We are not a perfect family, none are, but I am convinced that many of our problems occurred because we did not have the connection to our past and the comfort of knowing about our ancestors and their legacy that should have been handed down.

I have not received any encouragement from any of my immediate family members, mostly because they do not value or understand the importance of knowing from whom and from where we came.

You see this has been a mission of mine since I was nine years old. My brother James use to read about Africa. We would talk and dream about Africa but never in our wildest dreams did we dare think that one day one of us would visit the mother land as I did in February, 2010.

As legend has it, when I was a baby my uncle Otis who was the youngest son of Hiram and Gertrude was the greatest third baseman that had ever come through East St. Louis riding or walking. He was my chief baby sitter while my mother went to work cleaning white people's houses. He would carry me to baseball games in a bassinet. But during the summer of 1937, right after my second birthday which was one of the hottest days on record, Otis left me in the sun and I had a heat stroke.

I was hospitalized for over three months at Saint Mary's Hospital in East Saint Louis. Even though I had been critically ill when I returned home I was very sensitive to sound, sun and heat. It is a problem that continues to bother me to this day. I had to stay in the house most of the time and there were a lot of people always around making noise. I learned that the noise I was hearing was actually words. I kept hearing the same sound Cruise. I observed that everybody who lived in that house had the same sound; then I heard a different sound and only one person would respond until finally I realized that when I heard the word "Boone" they were talking to me.

For some reason I could not take my eyes off of the person who everybody called James. When he would look at me I always felt good. He became my best friend. For the next four years I had a new baby sitter.

Uncle Otis had volunteered for the Army. The things that James did and the stories that he told was so exciting. He would always find time to play with me and make sure that I had plenty of water. I had to drink a lot of water because of my illness. My parents were told to make sure that I drank a lot of water and James made sure that I did. To this day, I still drink at least a half gallon of water a day.

When school was out in the summer unlike most boys James' age he spent most of his free time with me; partly because I was not allowed in the sun for more than an hour at a time.

His favorite game was cowboys and Indians. He would cut off a broom stick and would play cops and robbers with me and my next youngest brother Howard. He seemed to always know how to entertain us.

I was excited about the idea of going to grade school. At that time the school yard ended on our property line. It took one minute to scurry past the softball field and run down the hall located on the bottom floor to Ms. Williams' classroom.

I felt at ease because my friend Charles Jefferson started at the same time as I did, and James who was in the third grade was directly across the hall in his classroom. I learned right away that I liked going to school. My mother had taught all of us how to read and write long before we started school. She taught us at home which gave us a head start over most of our classmates.

In addition to the normal curriculum we were taught about duty honor, and country. During my fifth grade year the war was ending but we continued to bring scrap metal and piled it on the school ground for the "War effort."

We were so enthusiastic the pile was as tall as some of the houses nearby. We were told that we were helping the war effort and we all believed it.

I had always played street ball with my brothers and realized that I could run, hit and catch with the best of them. I didn't know it at the time but I was becoming a better than average athlete. At school the girls played against the boys until we reached the sixth grade.

Believe it or not when we played a game against the girls, the boys lost more than they won. We had some tremendous female athletes. They could hold their own against anybody their age. They could all hit but the sluggers were Bessie Mae Cartwright, Nora Matory, Ernestine Harrison, and yes the mighty, Louise Burns. She would hit three or four home runs each time we played them.

When we reached the seventh grade the boys and girls would play teams from schools in East Saint Louis. The boys won more than they lost, but the girls beat every girl's team around. My years at Garrison were some of the best times of my life.

When I graduated from Garrison I recited President Lincolns' famous speech at Gettysburg. I felt like a giant that day and decided I wanted to speak to people about serious subjects and write speeches like President Lincoln.

My father was diagnosed with Tuberculosis in 1941, which eventually was the indirect cause of his death in 1949. James was the man of the house on those occasions when my father had to be admitted to the sanitarium. He was not the oldest, but he was dependable.

Although my mother did not complete her college work she taught black students in Dumas, Arkansas before she attended Lincoln. She was not qualified to teach in Illinois and like most colored women back then she began to have children one year after the next.

One of the greatest times I had with my father was the day that he learned that Mrs. Andrews was sick. She had been sick for over three weeks and the doctor was not able to help her. My father insisted that he could not only help her but would cure her.

After coming to see her for only a few minutes he took me to the nearby railroad tracks and pointed out a leaf from a tall plant that grew along the tracks called Mandrake leaves. He told me to pull the leaves from the tall stalks and fill the long sack that he left with me. He told me to bring them to Mr. Andrew's house which was located near the alley but on 40th Street, right behind the soft ball field at Garrison School.

What happened next was so astounding to a boy of nine; it is as clear to me as if it occurred yesterday. He had Mrs. Andrews removed from the small bed that she was lying in; she slept alone because she was afraid to sleep with her husband for fear that he would catch whatever she had.

My father placed a blanket on top of the first level of leaves directly on top of the mattress he then placed her back into the bed and covered her body with some of the Mandrake leaves; finally he placed a sheet on top and finished by covering the sheet with the remaining leaves. He then instructed her daughter Marie to give her mother as much water as she wanted, and as he walked out the door he said that he would return in about four hours.

When we returned about the time that the sun was going down the first thing that I noticed was a puddle of water beneath the bed. The bed was soaked and the leaves on top were very warm. When he began to remove the sheet he places it on the floor and put the leaves next to her body in the sheet. I touched the leaves and to my surprise they were very, very hot. So much so, that she had a few burn spots on her upper arms and her stomach. The leaves looked as if they had been boiled.

The mattress was as wet as if someone had poured a bucket of water on it. She was very weak for a few days but when we returned the third day she was sitting up and except for the burns on her arms she regained her health and lived for several years after that.

My father was not one to give you more than a dime at any one time but on this day he gave me a dollar from the five dollars that he charged Mr. Andrews for his service. Everybody in Centerville heard about how Fred Cruise had made Mrs. Andrews well. Even the teachers knew about it when I returned to school. I was proud that I was Boone Cruise the son of a hero albeit, for one day.

After that my father made a good living selling medicine to people in the community and the little money that he received from the scaled down pig business. He always had enough money, not a lot mind you, but enough.

He was able to help a lot of people recover from their sickness but could never figure out the medicine that would help him. He would mix different roots, some for pain and others for breathing but none of it worked for long. He hired my uncle Walter to harvest herbs from the woods around Centerville, and as far away as Sparta, Illinois, some thirty miles away.

As I look back I realize that I was happy as a child. I adored my father and mother. My father was a handsome man. He was about six feet two inches and he weighed about one hundred and seventy-five pounds. His complexion was a little darker than ocean sand mixed with white granules. His skin was very smooth. In fact smooth would be a very good description of him. Everything about him seemed effortless.

Everyone admired him for his good looks, his ready smile and his quick wit. He was intelligent and had the ability to make you feel good about yourself. You see he had a way of making people feel good without really giving them a reason why they should. He was able to do this with anyone even those who many people would consider as outcasts and bums.

My father worked mostly for himself; he sold ice in the summer and coal in the winter. Right after the war, he and two of his brothers bought a pig farm near the cemetery located just off Illinois Highway 159 in Centerville, Illinois. At first they did quite well until they could no longer feed the pigs the left-over food that they collected from restaurants in the area. In the pass they had been allowed to reheat the food but finally the health department required all farmers to feed the pigs either corn or some other kind of feed.

Prior to that time, it was not uncommon for them to take one hundred hogs to market every other month. In addition to his day job my father along with my uncle Henry continued to make herbal medicine for people who were suffering from every ailment you could think of. Uncle Henry started to make and dispense medicine commercially without a license which eventually landed him in jail.

My father was an unusual man in many ways because he cut his own trail. Even when he was dressed in a suit he never wore socks. It was just a quirk with him. He was a stately and elegant man so erect and yet he always appeared to be comfortable. He could make a stage production by the way in which he crossed his legs and how he would use his slender hands when he talked as if he was conducting an orchestra. Yes, my father was quite the looker.

Although my father and mother were as different as coffee and cream, together they did what I consider an admirable job in raising their children under some trying circumstances. One thing that galvanized this fact was what happed when we lost the house that we were living in at the time.

My grandfather bought the house when they arrived in 1927. After my grandmother died my grandfather refused to stay in the house and moved to a house at 3903 Tudor Avenue.

We received a notice saying that the house was to be auctioned because the taxes were not paid. I am not sure why this happened after all, my grandfather paid cash for the house when he arrived in 1927. The same house that he and my grandmother Gertrude lived in until her death in 1935.

I don't know for sure but I believe that the house was still in my grandfather's name. Whatever the reason, we were notified that we had thirty days to move or we would be tossed out on the street.

My mother never lost faith. She prayed to God with assurance that He would answer. I recall that she confided in my aunt Ceola from whom she drew additional strength. It was aunt Ceola who did everything she could to encourage her.

One week later my father was released from the hospital for the second time in three years. He immediately took action. He and his friend and former partner, Mr. Bill Fields built what I believe to be the first pre fabricated house in America. Where and how he came up with this idea to build a house in less than two weeks was pure genius. I now understand that it is a family trait to take nothing and turn it into something.

He purchased five salvaged railroad cars and took the top and sides off and sold the axles and wheels as scrap metal. Mr. Bill and my father owned a long wheeled base truck that they used to transport the parts of our new house to the vacant lot right next to Mr. Bill's house.

My father asked Mr. Bill what his address was and he said "1116 S 43d Street," my father then said, "Well our address is 1118 South 43rd Street." You see in those days box cars were eighty percent wood making it a lot easier to convert them into living space as compared to the metal box cars of today.

The lot where the house was built had been used to dump unused items of furniture and other non perishable items. And, to our knowledge no one owned the land; it may have belonged to the railroad because the house stood no less than fifteen feet from the tracks where trains still ran about five times a month. They used every piece of material from the trains and with the exception of the back porch the house was finished in record time. I can still see the back porch that was never completed because they ran out of wood.

On day one they dug a four foot wide trench that was two feet deep; they proceeded to put the railroad ties side by side, then stacked them three high. Afterwards they took several strips of metal to shore up and anchored the ties to steady the foundation.

On the second and third day they installed the floor and began to erect the sides making sure to put the windows or opening in their original place which they later framed out as windows and doors.

On day four they hired a hay picker to lift the roof onto the cross beams in order to connect the roof to the walls. The next morning they completed all of the tie downs and began to put roofing paper on the house. On the fifth day we moved into our new home, bought and paid for with less than four hundred dollars. My mother began to put up wall paper using a mixture of flour, glue, and water. I can still remember the smell of this most efficient concoction and the rose pattern that was so common in those days. My parents both worked tirelessly to make sure that we had a place to live.

He made it a house but she made it a home. Everyone who came by could not believe that just five days earlier it was a dump that was turned into a livable house and it was our home. We lived there for three years until a historic flood over ran the Mississippi River; and here it is sixty years later I can still remember the house.

The house was forty feet long and twenty feet wide which allowed them to set the floor from the trains and rivet it in place without making any cuts. Our new house was half as wide as it was long. It was what we called a shot gun house you could aim down the hallway from the front all of the way to the back. The rooms were ten feet in length with a three foot hall that ran through each room. The only doors were the front and back doors. There was one window on the street side, two on the north and south side, and one on the west end where the kitchen was located. As I said the address was 1118 S. 43rd Street and I am proud to have called it my home.

Our house was the last house that the community felt was on the correct side of the tracks. We looked down on the people who lived on the other side of the tracks; it still amazes me how people will perceive people as less fortunate when as in their case they brought a system of unity of family, and the desire to make their life better. A belief that many who came in the 1920's seemed to have lost.

Even today, many descendants from the last group have made a better life for themselves and continue to hold on to the belief that family is important. In fact, my brother Fred and many other young men who went to war in Korea returned and married many of the girls from across the track.

Reflecting on those halcyon days, I shudder at our lack of understanding as we just went along with the flow that societies' norms sent our way. These were people who by every measurement were headed in the right direction while we stood by and thought somehow we were superior to them.

A good example of this type of thinking which truly is really judging a book by its cover was a lesson we all learned taught to us by a young man who was simply known as Bubba. Bubba lived on the other side of the tracks. He was about twenty years old; he was six feet four inches tall with a dark complexion. He was quiet and kept mostly to himself. When he did speak he spoke in the vernacular of a person from the rural south. He mostly wore bib overalls, and brogan boots with no socks.

I personally didn't find him offensive and for the life of me could not understand why he offended my friends, especially the one who considered himself as the "bull of the woods" in the person of Joe Johnson, the starting fullback for Lincoln High School and the resident intimidator.

Joe was about six foot four and weighed approximately two hundred and twenty five pounds; he had a small waist, with shoulders that look as though he was wearing pads. He considered himself a ladies' man even though he wasn't good looking. He attracted his share of girls because he was a star athlete, and not because of his looks. In size both of them were book ends but were like coal and ice in temperament.

On this particular day we all gathered at Nick's pool hall as was our usual practice. Joe started to raze Bubba and talked about his mama. Unfortunately it had become a custom for Joe to harass and bully those that he viewed as lesser than he. In this case he made an unwise decision to include Bubba in this category.

Joe was dressed in a brown suit and Bubba was in his usual overalls. Bubba asked Joe to stop, what we called playing the dozens, this is when one talks about a person mother or female linage. Joe ignored Bubba's request and continued to do so with a smirk on his face and a renewed desire to offend. Bubba had taken enough and told Joe "If you don't stop I am going to bust you."

This was a challenge that Joe could not back down from. In fact, he was edged on by one of his cronies and cohorts, James Jefferson, Jr. who we called "Turkey Breast," because of his big protruding chest which made him look like a gobbler. It seemed that everybody had a nickname in Fireworks.

James convinced Joe to change clothes with him and when Joe came running out of the pool hall with his boxer's stance he was met by the shortest right hand since Joe Louis knocked out Max Smelling. The punch stopped Joe in his tracks and as he fought to stay on his feet he began to turn away as if to run, but instead landed among the empty cans and empty beer and whiskey bottles that had be thrown into the ditch which ran alone side of the pool hall. In less than an hour the whole town knew that Goliath had fallen.

Bubba went back to being his usual quiet and unassuming self. But he came alive when we began practicing for our local baseball team. It was unbelievable. I noticed that Bubba was standing with our manager and I heard him ask, "Can I chunk a few pitches?" At first Shelby Andrews, our manager didn't understand what he was saying but finally agreed more to humor him and get him out of the way than to actually see if he had any skills. As I said it was unbelievable. Bubba took the mound dressed in his usual coveralls and brogans; he warmed up with about ten pitches and announced that he was ready. The first batter was Marvin Holden, our second baseman who was a contact hitter and rarely struck out, but after four pitches exclaimed "This is like trying to hit a pea in a snow storm." Bubba was throwing nothing but "smoke", smoke that none of us had witnessed before.

This enraged Joe who made himself the next batter. He stormed into the batter's box taking his stance with defiance and anger, and called for the first pitch. It didn't seem as if Bubba added any more effort into the pitch but it was much faster than the previous four. The sound of the ball hitting the catcher's mitt was the same as hearing a tree branch hitting the roof of a car.

It made a sharp, crisp, crackling sound and it sent electricity through us all. We all knew that Joe and nobody else would be able to hit Bubba. Even after such an outstanding audition we did not make an exception to our unspoken rule that no one from across the tracks would ever play on our team.

It wasn't until we played a game in Lincoln Park on a humid Sunday afternoon did we learn that Bubba was scheduled to pitch against us with our usual bravado, we tried to convince each other that we could beat him. He took the mound wearing one of the Colts jersey's over his bib overalls and his ever present brogans. He threw nothing but fast balls and began to mow us down like blades of grass.

One after another, one two three, you're out. I don't recall that anyone fouled one of his pitches, let alone hit him at all. Needless to say that after that performance we changed our rule and Bubba became the first player from across the tracks to join our team, and by far was our best player.

It was then and there that we began to slowly change our attitude about looking down on people from across the tracks. As I look back on that time now and I take into consideration the bigger picture of today's society. I now see how even then for such a small group as ours, sports plays a part as an icebreaker against prejudice.

This was exactly what happened in major league baseball over sixty years ago when Jackie Robinson broke the color barrier. Reflecting on those days, I shudder at our lack of understanding that we just went along with the flow our society sent our way.

After my father died we had to receive aid from the County Welfare Department. My mother received one hundred seventy five dollars per month. She earned an extra one hundred dollars a month by doing day work.

My mother was a beautiful dark brown skin stately woman and was very athletic; she stood almost six feet tall and was not afraid to defend her children from the dangers of the neighborhood bullies. I recall a time when a young man hit my older brother; she came down to Mr. Green's store on the corner of 41st and Piggott Avenue. The fight lasted about one minute, one punch, and he was out cold.

The store sat upon a foundation of mortar and brick columns spaced about six feet apart. The floor stood about three feet from the ground. Before I knew what had happened the bully was partially underneath the store with his feet almost completely hidden and his chest and head was beyond the edge of the store. What a punch!

You might say that she had actually knocked him for a loop. It was during that brief encounter that I realized that she was the boss and had the tools to back it up. She pointed her finger at him as he began to realize what had happened and said, "If you ever dream of hitting one of my children again you had better leave town."

The thing that I remember most about my mother was her strength and courage. You could say I was in awe of her. There has not been one day in my life that my love for her has not increased. I love my memories of her as much as I did the woman herself; she stood so tall and strong on this earth. She was a proud woman. She instilled pride in each and every one her children and quite simply I loved the fact that she was my mother.

She taught us how to clean the house, wash clothes and do the dishes. She also taught us how to treat a woman. She always said "Never put your hands on a woman. And, before you marry any woman, if her mother is alive, spend some time around her and her husband, and you will know what to expect if you decide to marry her." She added with her infectious smile, "you will also get a good idea of how your bride to be will look later in life."

A year after my father's death, my mother married Mr. Cleveland Brown, Sr. but only after telling us that she had known him and his wife who he had divorced five years earlier. She went on to say that he worked for Monsanto Chemical and would be a good provider for us. The first time I saw him he rode up in his 1948 Chrysler loaded down with groceries.

It was a glorious time we had a car to ride in and a generous supply of food and went to Sears on our first shopping spree. Mr. Brown drank on weekends but he was a quiet drinker. To our complete surprise we got an unexpected Christmas present when Cleveland Brown, Jr. was born in December of 1950. We had a new baby in the house and to say that Mr. Brown bragged about his new son would be an understatement.

Wednesday, January 11, 1893

Mr. & Mrs. F.M. Apperson of Scranton sent us a fruit cake & some pecans.
Rev. M.F. Harmon has been elected Chaplain of the Penitentiary.
Col. L.N. Moore, Winona merchant, died suddenly Tuesday of heart disease.
B. Ambrose, Italian Tunica merchant, was murdered in his store Christmas eve.
Mr. Lea of Amite Co. who killed Wm. Cutrer was pronounced insane.
Chas. O. Summers & Tom Murray robbed the Meridian Express Co. Dec. 6th.
Greenville Treasurer Alexander was ordered by the Board of Supervisors to produce the county funds of $50,000., so brought the money in a wagon.
Mrs. John McVey whose husband, a R.R. employee, was killed in a train wreck near Holly Springs, has sued the R.R. Co. for $50,000. in a West Point court.
Trustee's Notice: J.A. Jennings, Trustee appointed by F.A. Jordan in place of A.J. Hand, to sell the land of A. & M.E. Lewis: NW4 NW4, W2 SW4, SW4 sec.7 T3 R13 & NE4 SW4, E2 SW4 NE4 sec.7 T3 R12 & W2 NW4 sec.12 T3 R12 & SE4 SE4, NW4 SW4 sec.1 T3 R12.
Mr. Pearson of Taylorville was in town yesterday.
J.T. Brown & Dick Benison are in Meridian today.
M.D. Parker called at our office last Monday.
D.G. Burnett was in town yesterday.
Ex-Treasurer S.G. Graham was at the Courthouse yesterday.
Jno. Street, our printer, is on the sick list.
Mrs. S.F. Thigpen, who has been very ill, is on the road to recovery.
Mr. Gus Harmon has been visiting his sister, Mrs. S.S. Cope.
Monroe Massey was in town with 984 lbs. of pork which he sold for 6 cts. a lb
A.J. Hutto, Montrose mill man & merchant, & family spent the holidays with relatives in Ellisville.
Eugene Bondarant, salesman for S.S. Cope, has accepted a position as book keeper for Turner Bros. of Vossburg.

Supervisors appoint road overseers & workers for the next year

Aaron Page	Sam Crosby	Will Knight	Gabe Thigpen
Daub Moffat	R. Hosey Jr.	W.I. Rogers	W.E. Thigpen
L.M. Yelverton	Ab Denson	A.J. Herrington	J.O. Denson
Roderick McFarland	Bob Gaddy	March Dease	Tom Dease
Adam Dease	J.B. Thigpen	Jep Thigpen	E.A. Campbell
W. Herrington	E.A. White	Henry Husbands	N.L. Hudson
W. Herrington	E.K. Taylor	H.P. Cook	J.A. Morris
C. Thornton	Bishop Nixon	J.P. Browder	Jerry Nelson
erry Hogan	Geo. Risher	C.L. Nixon	J.D. Lee
scar Baker	J.S. Turner	Louis Lynum	G.A. Terral
llis Garner	Lance Carmichael	Jim Cruise	Joe Lindsey
	Paupers		
ry Sarter	Christiana Blackwell		
ttie Sampson	Becky Walley	Ben Blackwell	Jacob Davis
ll Cole	Debbie Lewis	Irene Read	Lydia Rogers
V Porter		Mollie Flynn	Mary Abney

Wednesday, January 18, 1893

. Beall, formerly of West Point, killed F.R. McKinnon at Guthree, OK.
es Seymour of Scranton died in New Orleans last week.
s Mary Sanders will soon be admitted to practice law at Corinth.
.Buchannan, Holly Springs merchant, was crushed by a train at Tupelo.
Gertrude Theiages? died in Meridian last week from poison sardines.

Jun Cruise appointed as a supervisor of road crew

121

CHAPTER 20

THEY SAY THAT THEY COME IN THREES

I remember the day that my grandfather died. In fact I went to see him the day before. I was thirteen years old and I still felt intimidated by my grandfather. I loved him but I was scared to talk to him. I had so many questions that I wanted to ask him, but for some reason I was always afraid to do so.

The day before he died he was seated in his chair near the rear door. I went over to see if he needed me to bring in some coal for his heater. It was a cold windy day and the clouds were blocking what little sun that was in the sky. I asked how he was feeling; one of the few questions that I could get out without stuttering.

He looked at me with his coal dark eyes; the ones which I felt were always looking through me. With a wry smile on his face he said he was just fine, but he did have a burning in his chest. He went on to say that he would go and see Dr. Eubanks if he didn't feel any better the next day. Unfortunately he died the next day.

I am not sure who brought us the news, but I do remember aunt Adelaide (The girl pictured on the back cover of this book) was talking to the undertaker and another man from the health department. I only wish that I had talked more with my grandfather and asked him about his life in Mississippi. Had I done so, I would have found out about my grandmother Gertrude and how she and my grandfather had come from Mississippi in 1927. This was after my grand uncle William had been murdered in the streets of Paulding, Mississippi. I would have learned that this is why my grandfather first made the decision to move.

I would have learned that my grandfather kept his promise that he made to William and sent his wife Anna and their children Richard and Anna to California. They left a week after William's funeral. A funeral that was by all accounts the largest funeral of any colored man in all of Jasper County.

His casket was taken to the grave yard in a caisson drawn by two white horses, which was loaned to them by a rich white business man from Heidelberg. They say that the procession line behind it was at least a quarter mile long. They buried my grand uncle William in the Spring Hill Cemetery beside his brother Joseph and my great grandparents James and Hannah Cruise.

Had I talked to my grandfather I am sure that he would have told me about the loan that he made prior to leaving Mississippi and the true meaning behind it, which I believe was to establish ownership of his land. Land his father had given him and land on which he worked to support his family.

He would have shared how he had observed many people having their land taken from them and he wanted this documentation to prove that his family owned their land. I would have understood how this land was part of the very fiber that tied our family together, just as much as the blood that we share.

He and Gertrude finally moved to the "Land of Lincoln" in late 1927, along with his children most of whom were grown and married; Chester, Fred, Hiram, Jr., Walter, Horace, Otis, and Adelaide. He went from being a businessman in the south to a man with too many bad memories that haunted him until the day he died. His move had been deliberate and final. He never set foot in Mississippi again.

Seven years before my grandmother's death, my grandfather and his children dedicated themselves to taking care of what mattered most to them, Gertrude; who grew progressively ill as time went by. She lost her battle with stomach cancer in 1935. It is my belief that in the end it was her death that he could no longer endure. As I said, these are things that I learned after many and much research into our families' history.

Since I was only thirteen years old at the time, the only thing that I remember about my grandfather's funeral was the little church on 40th street that was so poor they didn't have a piano. The casket was placed between a center post and the pulpit. You had just enough room to squeeze by as you viewed the body.

Although it was sixty two years ago, in my mind's eye I still remember the faces at his service. Every Cruise and Foggy that I recall being alive at that time were present. That is everyone except for my grandfather's oldest son, my Uncle Henry.

A few months after my grandfather's death my father began to get weaker, and weaker. You could see this in everything that he did. He no longer stood as straight or talked with his hands as much. You could hear the weakness in his voice. He eyes seemed dim and not focused with their usual sharpness.

As I think back on it now, I could tell that he was in pain and was slowly slipping away. He decided that he would have a new experimental operation that was being conducted at Barnes Hospital in Saint Louis, Missouri.

I knew that my father was sick but I had no idea that the surgery was high risk. He understood the possible outcome but had made up in his mind that death was better for him than the constant pain he was enduring. I was told that he was going to have an operation and would have to stay in the hospital for a week. He died on the operating table. It was just before his birthday in 1949.

I was fourteen years old and I felt so alone. I had no one to confide in and due to my confused state of mind I was angry and hurt because I knew so little about my father's life as a boy. Any chance of learning about my family's rich history was lost. The three men who meant the most to me were gone, my brother James, my grandfather Hiram and my father Frederick Douglas Cruise.

I never thought to ask my uncles and aunts. I now know that it is critical for fathers and grandfathers to tell their sons and grandsons about the things that they faced in life as young men. It will help them to connect with their ancestors, and help them to feel a part of someone more than themselves.

And it is just as important for descendants to ask about their families' past history. I know that had I known this, it would have helped me with my identity crisis.

Unlike it is today, when I was a child it was very uncommon for a household not to include both mother and father. Not only were there two parents in the household, but in most cases the father was the head of the household in every way. He was not only the bread winner but he also served as the director of the family.

He was the chief disciplinarian. He gave direction to the family and made sure that each member had a goal in life. One of the most asked questions from not only my father, and other adults was, what are you going to be when you grow up? None of us realized at the time that knowing or not knowing about the roles that our ancestors accomplished, played a major role in our answer.

As I said unfortunately today the term African American Father, and two parent households have become almost obsolete. It is not just uncommon, but sad to say it's the norm today. The mother serves not only as the head of the household but is the only parent involved in rearing the children. This is not just a sad commentary on today's society; it is not a statement of morality, it is the beginning of the end of the family, and that in itself is a reality. The family as we know it, or believe it should be has in most cases become a figment of our memory.

Life was especially difficult for me and seemed to change for the worst. I was still confused and angry. I felt as if my life was without purpose. I had no course in which to travel and the inner loneliness was almost unbearable. I still attended school each day in fact I never missed a day of school for the eight years that I attended Garrison Elementary.

I made good grades but I began to do things that never in my wildest dreams I thought I would do, let alone actually do them. I began to steal from my mother by taking my friends to the grocery store where we had a monthly account. I would get different kinds of sweets and luncheon meat and yes, a few packets of Kool Aid. This behavior continued until my mother received a call from the owner who informed her of what I was doing.

I thought that she would never stop beating me. Although the whipping hurt it was the truths that she explained during the onslaught that hurt the most. I thought back to the day when she knocked the young man out for hitting my brother and was glad that she used a belt instead of her fists. After this episode I turned my attention to other adult men, men who would spend time with me, and would give me advice based upon their experiences.

Most notably was my best friend's father, Mr. James Jefferson. I was attracted to him because he reminded me of my grandfather. They had some of the same features and they were about the same height and color, and had a similar demeanor and he was from Hazlehurst, Mississippi.

Other men included my uncle Chester, a man of great determination and resolve. He worked eighteen years for the Illinois Central Railroad where he worked as an engineer's helper until he got a job at the Aluminum-Ore manufacturing plant, the same company that Mr. Jefferson worked for on Missouri Avenue. My uncle Chester held the job until he died at the age of sixty five. Another person I looked up to was Charles Bozeman whom for some reason called me "Funny" instead of "Boone, like everyone else in my neighborhood. Mr. Bozeman was a man who would always make me feel good and told me I was going to amount to something one day.

He had a sister Mrs. Marie Bozeman Timmons who also played a significant role in my life. Mrs. Timmons, Rebo as we called her secretly, was the truancy officer for our school she was also our Cub Scout Leader. I remember spending many hours with her. She took the time to make me feel special.

Mrs. Timmons was always gracious and I will always remember her with a smile and how she was devoted to her husband whose name was Tom. She was the first woman who I saw driving a car, my mother was the second. She often took me to her church located in East Saint Louis. After service we would always have a great meal at the church.

I didn't realize it but my Uncle Walter had a positive influence on me. He would take me with him early in the morning to dig roots. We would work all day stopping only to drink water or to eat a light lunch. He never talked about himself but talked about life in general terms. We would wash and dry the roots and place them on top of a tin shed that my grandfather built to stable his mule that died mysteriously around Christmas time in 1941. It was reported all around town that Dib, my grandfather was tired of feeding the mule because he would not work. So he gave the mule a little poison. Everybody started calling us Dib, Dib, the mule killer. We had no idea that this "nick name was given to him as a young man.

After the roots finished drying, my uncle Walter would sell some to my father and the remainder to my uncle William Henry; who by this time was dispensing medicine from his office in down town East Saint Louis. As far as I can remember my uncle Henry practiced medicine from his office. I thought he was a doctor because that is what everybody called him. It wasn't until he was convicted on two separate occasions for distributing medicine without a license did I find out that he was not a doctor. Practicing medicine without a license is a federal offence and he spent some time in Federal Prison for breaking the law.

Dr. Miles Davis, Jr. had an office on fifteenth and Broadway across the hall from my uncle. His son Miles Davis, III went on to become a legendary jazz musician, and one of the most prominent jazz musicians of his time. His father who was a trained veterinarian took care of humans as well as any medical doctor. Although we never went to him it was a well known secret that he was as good, if not better, than any other doctor in town.

I was thirteen years old when I graduated from the all black Garrison School. Staffed by the greatest teachers and educators I have ever known. They were all excellent and caring. Two of the teachers that stand out in my mind were my fifth grade teacher Ms. Morgan and Ms. King my eighth grade teacher.

Ms. King traveled all over the world during her school vacations. She brought the world to her classroom through pictures and the exciting stories; she shared picture so descriptive that you actually thought that you had traveled along with her. Her stories stirred my desires to see the world and one day travel to my homeland. I had no idea at the time that it would actually happen.

Ms. Morgan was a short stocky, dark skinned woman. She demanded that you work hard and not only respect yourself and your family's name but to respect the rights and opinions of others. She opened up the world of numbers and words to me. She also had a special way about her that made each class member feel that they were her special student.

I recall attending her funeral some years later and as I sat and thought about her I had a feeling of emptiness. I thought to myself, how grateful I was that this woman had played a great part in molding my character.

Ms. King did not live in our local community. Unfortunately I never found out what she did after her retirement partly because I was in the Army. I did travel to some of the places that she had visited and told us about when I was her student. As I reflect years later I understand that she not only allowed me to see the world but that she helped me discover through her patience and love how to gain my sense of self, and the feeling that I was somebody. For that I shall always be grateful.

In those days it was quite important, and I feel essential that schools were more of a community, a family if you will, an extended family. I felt that as if Garrison was a prime example of the Swahili saying, "It takes a whole village to raise a child." The teachers at Garrison not only helped us to see the world through their eyes but made it their mission and duty to open our eyes to see the world and its possibilities.

Ms. King traveled to California in 1949. She took pictures of Mt. Baldy with its snow capped mountains, in the summer time. I often travel Highway 210 through Pasadena. I think of her pictures and how the mountains were so high that snow remained atop them while at the same time it was warm in the valley. She helped me see the world with her pictures and now I see them with my own eyes.

Garrison prepared us not only for high school, but for life. One of the main reasons for its success was our Principle, Mr. Thomas J. Fagan, who attended Langston University in Lawton, Oklahoma; along with Ms. Williams, our first grade teacher, who was the first smiling face you saw on the first day of school.

Mr. Fagan was a strong educated no nonsense man. He was hard but he was fair. In those days, corporal punishment was the order of the day, and Mr. Fagan was a man who knew how to get the most of the ten self prescribed licks that he administered to the boys who broke the rules. He was also the Boy Scott leader for the first scout troop in our city. You didn't mess with Mr. Fagan.

On the other hand, Ms. Williams was a friendly gregarious woman who understood how to excite young minds in the pursuit of excellence. Leaving her class was an emotional experience but we left with the conviction that we would complete high school and maybe even attend college. She made you feel good to finally be a student. We knew our teachers because our older brothers always talked about school, and the teachers who they considered as mean and too demanding.

My first official "crush" was for Nora Matory who was the shoe repairman's daughter, and my fellow class mate. I believe the reason why I was first attracted to Nora was because of her beautiful dark red skin. Her skin had a glow about it that reminded me of my mother's. Maybe this is where the original attraction came from; you see hers' and my mother's skin had a uniqueness to it thought it was quite dark, it also included a reddish hue which made it look rich and full.

I was the Valedictorian and Nora was the Salutatorian. Our speeches were very emotional. They were about slavery, education, and the hope of the future.

Ms. King was aware of my deep feeling regarding Africa and wrote a speech for me, but at the last minute changed it to Lincoln' Gettysburg Address. She recalled how passionate I had been when we read the famous speech by President Lincoln.

Graduation night was the highlight of my young life. I was the star of the show and that was when I realized that I could communicate with people and transfer my passion to them. It is a God given talent that I have tried to refine since that eventful night at a simple grade school ceremony.

In Centerville there were only two public high schools that blacks could attend Love Joy High and Lincoln High. Lincoln was the oldest it was established in 1909.

Love Joy was the choice of students who lived in Centerville because of the cost of transportation. Students who attended Lincoln had to use public transportation while those who attended Love Joy were transported by school bus.

The better athletes went to Lincoln which is where I would have gone had I attended public school. I attended St. Mary's Catholic School because I believed that I would receive a better education and because I thought Nora was going to attend.

Shortly before school started Saint Teresa's Academy opened its doors to black girls. Nora decided to go there which broke my heart. Two years later Central Catholic an all male school moved to their newly constructed building. They changed their name to Assumption High School and followed Saint Teresa's example and opened their doors and began to admit Black male students.

My two years at St. Mary's was a blur. I was beginning to look at girls seriously but none of them looked back at me. I was short for my age and had an eye on a nice girl named Kirby Lucky. She was short and had long wavy hair; she lived in an area about three miles south of Centerville near the only golf course that black people could play. For some reason it was called Golden Gardens.

I finally got the nerve to ask her if I could walk her home, for six months I walked her close to her house and make the return trip in less than an hour. She finally told me that her father did not want me or any other boy to talk to her. We became friends and she is now retired and living somewhere in "Middle America."

St. Mary's didn't have any athletic teams, and our only physical exercise was square dancing. I still remember the call of the Texas Star, and the doe se does. Two of the Hawkins girls, Mary Lee and Burley, were students with me. Burley married my brother Fred Douglas, Jr. after he returned from the Korean War.

Fred had a scientific mind and wanted to become a chemist but because of his experiences in the war, when he returned he was never the same. The war had done some terrible things to him as it has to so many in the past and continue to do so presently.

After several failed attempts at college, Fred resigned himself to prepare his children for higher learning. He educated them at home; he was a teacher's dream because his homework was more rigorous than taking exams at school. His children were always at the top of their class. After enduring years of physical excruciating pain accompanied by extreme mental strain, he succumbed to his injuries and died in 1980.

At St. Mary's we were required to attend mass daily. One day our altar boy Eugene Parnell was sick. Father Burke motioned for me to come into the side room to help with the mass. I kept insisting that I was a Baptist. He seemed not to understand, or care. I was nervous, but I steadied myself and said with a strong voice, "Father I am not a Catholic, I am a Baptist." His eyes grew wide when he realized the ridiculous situation we were in. His grew beet red. He straightened himself and said as dignified as he could, "I am sorry Matthew I can do it alone. As he turned away he asked over his shoulder with a puzzled look on his face, "how is it then that you are able to recite the altar boy's responses?" I stood as straight as I could and exclaimed, Father, I hear the response five days a week; everybody should be able to recite the altar boy's part as well as yours.

The beginning of my junior year my life went through a distinctive change. St. Mary's closed without notice. The ironic thing about its closing, twentyseven of the thirty boys who had attended St. Mary's was Catholics and they transferred to public schools. But only three attended the newly built Assumption High School, Charles Jefferson, Charles Radford and me, and we were Non-Catholics.

I came into my own during my final two years of High School. My Friend Charles Jefferson played on the baseball team and Charles Rayford was the star of the basketball team. I played on the football and golf teams. These were fun years. We were the only black athletes in a predominately white school. In fact, we were the only blacks in the whole school.

This created some comical and unusual events during my years at Assumption. In Centerville everybody played football. In fact, when I say everybody in Firework Station played football, I mean girls as well as boys. There were some girls who played the game better than some boys. There was Bessie Mae Cartwright who was about my height at the time. The other being Louise Burns who in contrast to Bessie Mae was a bruiser; Bessie Mae was as fast as grease lighting.

I scored twenty eight touchdowns while playing two years of football at Assumption. Had Bessie Mae gone out for our high school team, she would have possibly been the first girl to play a skill position, and with our line would have scored forty. As I said, everyone in Centerville played football, and I do mean everybody.

For this reason, I decided to go out for the football team. I still remember the first day I brought color to the all white locker room. The guys were standing around, slapping towels, and doing the things jocks do before and after practice.

The moment that I walked in all eyes instantly went on me, the joking stopped as the locker room grew silent. I could feel their stares coming from every direction. As I sat down on the bench to put on my practice uniform I could feel their stares growing more intense; first I removed my shirt then my shoes; I could see that everyone in the locker room was leaning in closer to get a look at my genitals. Some leaned to the left and others to the right, but it was quite clear what they were looking for.

As I removed my under wear I believe everyone took a step forward. I laughed, and said "guys it's all a myth." Instantly the tension was broken, we all laughed, and I was accepted as part of the team. You might say I had passed another test.

I played two sports, football and golf. I was the starting half back. I also returned kickoff and punt returns. I was also a defensive back. We played predominately white Catholic Schools. I was the only black on either side of the ball. I recall one game in particular, in which we played against Central Catholic High School in Bloomington, Illinois a farming community.

You know how rabid small town high school football fans can be. Often communities like these, have just one high school. The whole city shuts down to support their local team. In the mid-west where I grew up football was king by far.

Often grandfathers, fathers, and sons played for the same school. It was this hostility and dedication to their team that I was going to face. For me, it was just another game. It seemed to me for them it was a matter of life and death; let alone racial pride. As we approached the city we were glad to see some buildings because we had passed through endless miles of corn fields. After we arrived at the stadium I was immediately greeted with hostility and racial aggression.

A white man dressed in bib overalls, a straw hat with a flush red face verbally attacked me the moment that I stepped off the bus he said, "So, you are the nigger that's been scoring all of those touchdowns." I wanted to applaud him, for being so astute, and picking me out of the crowd. He went on to say, "My son is the quarterback of this team and we have not lost a game in three years; and if you think you are going to come up here and beat us you have another think coming. You had better not score one touchdown because if you do something bad is going to happen to you. I will be watching you." One of my coaches stepped in between us and pushed the man aside. I shrugged my shoulders and thought no more about it.

It was a cold crisp Northern Illinois evening a few weeks before Thanksgiving. I was concerned that I may not be able to see the ball in time because there was a slight fog, coupled with the bright lights that had given me some problems while trying to catch the ball during our warm up time.

I looked around for the man who had accosted me when I came off the bus. My attention moved back on the field where the referee was blowing the whistle to start play. We had set the play to start up the middle and form a lane where I could cut to the right. As I caught the ball and started up field I could see that the play had a chance to work as planned because their pursuit was in the center of the field. Without being touched, I found the end zone eighty seven yards later.

As I was leaving the field I spotted my new adversary standing on the other side of the track that encircled the football field. I again turned my attention to the game and I scored two more touch downs before the half. The score was twenty four to nothing, and my coach saw no need for me go back into the game. When half time arrived we headed for the locker room to plan strategy for the second half.

As I ventured down the runway to the locker room I was surprised by a sucker punch to my right eye; it was my new adversary who had hit me. A grown man about forty to forty five six feet tall weighing about two hundred pounds.

Although I was sixteen years old, five feet six inches tall and weighted one hundred sixty pounds with my uniform on, I was staggered and stunned but I never lost my feet; in fact I had my full faculties about me. My adversary said, "I told you not to score any touch downs boy." I heard him say "now what are you going to do about that?" I replied "I am going to try and not allow you to hit me in my left eye." He was immediately subdued and removed from the stadium.

Another memory that makes me smile even today was our annual trek to the Arch Diocese. Every year the Jesuit Brothers would take the entire school to the Diocese in Bellville, Illinois. We were lined up to kiss the Bishop's ring but when my turn came I shook his hand instead; his look of disbelief was only heighten by my response as I pulled my hand from his surprisingly strong grip, and exclaimed, "I am a Baptist." He smiled and said, "that alright my son we are all God's children."

STATE OF MISSISSIPPI

MISSISSIPPI STATE DEPARTMENT OF HEALTH
VITAL RECORDS

ANY ALTERATION OR ERASURE VOIDS THIS CERTIFICATE

1 PLACE OF DEATH

County Jasper

Vot. Pct. Garners Mill

Inc. Town or Village or City .... (No. .... St.; .... Ward) If death occurred in a hospital or institution give its NAME instead of street and number.

STATE OF MISSISSIPPI
STATE BOARD OF HEALTH
Bureau of Vital Statistics
CERTIFICATE OF DEATH

6071

Registration District No. 9682

Primary Registration District No. 9682

File No. ....

Registered No. 12

2 FULL NAME Joseph Henry Crusie

PERSONAL AND STATISTICAL PARTICULARS

3 SEX Male

4 COLOR or RACE Black

5 SINGLE, MARRIED, WIDOWED, OR DIVORCED (Write the word) Married

6 DATE OF BIRTH Sept (Month) 20 (Day), 1875 (Year)

7 AGE 37 yrs. 8 mos. 20 ds. If LESS than 1 day ...... hrs. or ...... min.?

8 OCCUPATION (a) Trade, profession, or particular kind of work Farmer

(b) General nature of industry, business, or establishment in which employed, (or employer) ....

9 BIRTHPLACE (State or Country) Miss

PARENTS

10 NAME OF FATHER James Crusie

11 BIRTHPLACE OF FATHER (State or Country) Georgia

12 MAIDEN NAME OF MOTHER Hanna Reid

13 BIRTHPLACE OF MOTHER (State or Country) Miss

14 THE ABOVE IS TRUE TO THE BEST OF MY KNOWLEDGE

(Informant) Charley Crusie

(Address) Paulding, Miss

15 Filed 4/30 1914 C.N. Garner Registrar

MEDICAL CERTIFICATE OF DEATH

16 DATE OF DEATH 4 (Month) 29 (Day), 1914 (Year)

17 I HEREBY CERTIFY That I attended the deceased from ...., 191..., to ...., 191..., that I last saw h...... alive on ...., 191..., and that death occurred on the date stated above, at ......m.

The CAUSE OF DEATH * was as follows:

Assassinated

No Physician

Duration ...... yrs. ...... mos. ...... ds.

Contributory (SECONDARY) .... Duration ...... yrs. ...... mos. ...... ds.

Signed .... M. D.

.... 191... Address ....

*State the DISEASE CAUSING DEATH, or, in death from VIOLENT CAUSES, state (1) MEANS OF INJURY; and (2) whether ACCIDENTAL, SUICIDAL, or HOMICIDAL.

18 LENGTH OF RESIDENCE (For Hospitals, Institutions, Transients, or Recent Residents)

At Place of death ...... yrs. ...... mos. ...... ds. In the State ...... yrs. ...... mos. ...... ds.

Where was disease contracted, if not at place of death? ....

Former or usual residence ....

19 PLACE OF BURIAL OR REMOVAL Spring Hill Cemetery

DATE OF REMOVAL ...., 191...

20 UNDERTAKER Geo. Mayers

ADDRESS Paulding, Miss

Form V. S. No. 4. 75 M. 8-27-12. T.

ANY ALTERATION OR ERASURE VOIDS THIS CERTIFICATE

THIS IS TO CERTIFY THAT THE ABOVE IS A TRUE AND CORRECT COPY OF THE CERTIFICATE ON FILE IN THIS OFFICE

NOV 20 2003

Judy Moulder
STATE REGISTRAR

WARNING: A REPRODUCTION OF THIS DOCUMENT RENDERS IT VOID AND INVALID. DO NOT ACCEPT UNLESS EMBOSSED SEAL OF THE MISSISSIPPI STATE BOARD OF HEALTH IS PRESENT. IT IS ILLEGAL TO ALTER OR COUNTERFEIT THIS DOCUMENT.

VERIFY PRESENCE OF WATERMARK HOLD TO LIGHT TO VIEW

CHAPTER 21

A SHIP WITHOUT A RUDDER

As I approached my high school graduation, I felt like a ship without a rudder. I had no father but God. My mother was not astute enough or experienced enough to help guide me through the confusing process of grants and scholarships. I was so naive I thought that you had to be rich or get a scholarship to attend college. I did not have a counselor at Assumption and I was left to figure out what to do about furthering my education. I had one discussion with Mr. Fagan and he mentioned a black college as a possible choice. But, I had my heart set on going to a large school. I was left to fend for myself.

I didn't know what to do; I believed my high school coach George Martz when he told me that I had an inside track to go to his alma mater Norte Dame University in South Bend, Indiana. Although he didn't promise me anything, he told me that the university had scouted me along with a few other schools; such as Xavier University in Cincinnati, Ohio.

Coach Martz told me that Norte Dame was looking to bring in their first black running back. I really hoped that I would get this opportunity. This was the first time I actually considered going to college. As it turn out Norte Dame liked everything about me except I was not a Catholic. They chose a young man from New Jersey by the name of Aubrey Lewis who went on to have quite a successful career at Norte Dame and became one of the first black FBI agents.

After my disappointment of not going to college, I decided to join the service. I saw no real opportunities in East Saint Louis, and I knew no one who had the kind of job that I wanted. All of my brothers before me had gone to the service. By this time I had fallen in love with the first girl who actually paid any attention to me. Her name was Kathryn Hicks. We met at our local dance hall just before school started my senior year in 1953.

Kathryn was a year older than me. She was no taller than a mid-sized bar stool. She had a boyfriend whose name was William Ward but everyone called him "Mickey." He was well over six feet three and weighted about one hundred and forty five pounds; if you looked at him sideways you could not see him. Kathryn said that she and Mickey had broken up the previous week and he was giving her a hard time about it. Although I was short I weighed almost as much as Mickey so I had no fear of him.

I rescued her by asking her to dance. I embraced her as we did in those days, hug and move your feet every now and then. I noticed immediately that though she was shorter than me she was well built. She had all of the physical attributes that I had fantasized about; big legs, big hips, and big busts, all the things that I counted as physical beauty, to include the color of her reddish brown skin.

We dated our final year of high school; she graduated in January and I in graduated in June. I told her that I was going to the Army but before I graduated I asked her to marry me after I completed my basic training. We were married on July 11, 1954, and the following April our first child was born. Kathryn named her April Marie but she died two week later while sleeping in her crib.

Kathryn never really recovered from April's death. Our marriage was never the same and she lost all interest in attending college, or for that matter ever facing reality again. We remained married for eleven years. I still loved her but she began to suffer from Paranoid Schizophrenia. She was diagnosed after someone tried to attack her one month after she arrived in Hawaii.

We had a little apartment right outside the gate at Schofield Barracks, Hawaii. Someone tried to break into the apartment and she jumped from the second floor and landed on the concrete sidewalk.

At the time of the break in I was in the field on maneuvers. Before I could get back to Schofield I received word that she had been admitted to the hospital in Honolulu for injuries she suffered because of her jump to safety. When I got to the hospital I was surprised to learn that she had been committed to the mental ward.

Two weeks later she was sent to Fitzsimmons Army Hospital in Denver, Colorado for the mentally ill. I was transferred to the nearest Army post at Fort Carson, Colorado, located a few miles from Colorado Springs. After undergoing treatment for three months she was released and we rented a house in Colorado Springs.

At first things were fine. I was selected to play on the Installation baseball team where Billy Martin from the New York Yankees was the coach. Charley Pride of country western fame, George Altman who later played for the Chicago Cubs, Leon Wagner and Willie Kirkland both of whom played for the San Francisco Giants after completing there service commitment. We were loaded with talent. I played third base because Coach Martin liked my knowledge of the game and my love for the privilege of playing.

We won the All Service Championship against the Air Force. Prior to the series that was held in Nebraska, we played three games against a prison team in Canyon City. After traveling about fifty miles I heard the strangest thing, a black man, Charlie Pride singing with our catcher Bobby Gene Green. After he finished I told George who was seated next to me that Charlie could make a living singing country music one day. The rest is history.

Money was tight because I had purchased a house in East Saint Louis and had to pay rent in Colorado. As I was trying to figure out how we could survive I learned that Kathryn was pregnant with our second child. Kathryn seemed happy in part because she wanted another child, and partly because we decided that I would re-enlist for duty in Korea. It was the only way I would be allowed to sign up for another six years because we needed the money to move her back home. Her mother moved into our house and lived with Kathryn until my sixteen month tour in Korea was over. On November 11, 1957, I received a telegram that Matthew Jonathan Cruise was born on November 10, 1957. I had a son and our family's name would continue for another generation. I longed to go home but I had no choice but to remain until November 15, 1958. I missed my son's first birthday by twenty days. I was moving up in rank because I was an excellent golfer, coached our Brigade basketball team and played on our baseball team. It was during this time that I met William "Bill" Kunkel a skinny blond haired blue eyed white boy from Hoboken, New Jersey.

Our barracks were assigned before we arrived at Headquarters Company, 1st Brigade, 7th Infantry Division, at Camp Casey, South Korea. As was often the case because my name was Cruise the platoon sergeant thought I was a Cuban. He assigned me to a hut that was mostly occupied by whites. The minute that I walked in I knew that I was not wanted. Somebody shouted from behind a locker, "what do you want boy?" And from nowhere appeared this little swaggering young man who looked no more than seventeen said that he would take care of anybody who said another word.

We became friends until he completed his hitch in the Army. Bill was a fierce competitor who was an excellent point guard on my basketball team. I was surprised when I found out that he was going to play baseball for me. I was equally surprised when he told me that he was a pitcher. He said that he was going to play for the New York Yankees someday.

Sure enough, although he was not overpowering but had pin point control, I was not surprised to see him as a relief pitcher for the Kansas City Royals, and later with the Yankees. He went on to be

a great umpire in the major leagues, and a basketball referee in the National Basketball Association. He was flamboyant, yet steady, I still remember him as that young brash young man in Korea
.

My fortunes turned the summer before I completed my tour in Korea. I was in the habit of taking a seven iron that I cut down to fit into my duffle bag and took it everywhere I went, whether it was Hawaii or Korea. I also carried along twenty golf balls in two socks. Every Sunday morning I would hit golf balls in an open field. The third time out a ram-rod straight man came walking across the field. He was wearing a khaki tee shirt highly spit shined boots and a pair of khaki pants that stood as straight as he.

As he came closer I could tell that he was an officer even though he was not wearing any insignia. He said that he had been watching me, and wanted to know if I ever miss hit a shot. I said sir, I have been playing this game for most of my life, and no sir, I don't miss many. That was the day that I met Major General William F. Cunningham. As God would have it his administrative assistant was a man from my hometown Chief Warrant Officer Thomas Leggs.

The following week I was transferred to Headquarters, 7th Infantry Division with assignment to the Personnel Office. Since I was an excellent typist I was assigned as one of the soldiers who typed the orders issued by Division Headquarters.

The real reason I was assigned was our weekly helicopter trip to Soul to play against one of General Cunningham's old rival General Isaac D. White who was the Commanding General of all Army Forces in Korea. We never lost. Here I was an enlisted man playing with these powerful men who in spite of the difference in our rank, and our color, I was accepted and made comfortable in their presence. General Cunningham was a soldier liken to General Custer, emotional, strong willed, and a man of action. He would bend, but never break the rules. It was due to his guidance and encouragement that I started taking college courses while still in service, and later, he also insisted that I apply for a direct appointment as a Warrant Officer.

1866 STATE CENSUS JASPER COUNTY, MISSISSIPPI

Head of Household	MALES										FEMALES									
	10 & Under	10 to 20	20 to 30	30 to 40	40 to 50	50 to 60	60 to 70	70 to 80	80 to 90	90 to 100	10 & Under	10 to 20	20 to 30	30 to 40	40 to 50	50 to 60	60 to 70	70 to 80	80 to 90	90 to 100
Eliza H. Round		1									2		1					1		
W. H. Hardy		1									3		1							
J. M. Bennett			1																	
J. C. Heidelberg, Jr.			1										2							
Dr. S. E. Casteel	2	2				1					2	1		1						
Mrs. Catherine Hall	2	1												1						
Colored in the town of Paulding in no person's employed on their premises																				
Sandy Chapman																				
Wiatt Nicholson																				
Ann Overstreet																				
Jack Bynum																				
James Clark																				
Alfred Cooper																				
White males and females																				
James H. Chapman		1			1						1	1	2	1						
J. B. Gough		4			1							1		1						
Jesse G. Hyde	1		1	1							2	1								
W. M. Brame	4			1							1		2	1						
A. J. Hyde	2	1		1										1						
PAGE 28 These colored males and females are not in any persons employ or on their premises																				
Frank Reid																				
James Cruise																				
William Hyde																				

186

CHAPTER 22

VIETNAM AND AFTER

The last time that I lived with Kathryn was doing my tour in Augsburg, Germany. By this time our daughter Carmen and our youngest Michael had joined our family. While I was stationed at Fort Hood, Texas our life was in constant turmoil.

Kathryn did not trust any Germans and stayed inside our Senior Enlisted Quarters most of the time. I tried to make our life as normal as possible but it was a difficult time for all of us. Finally Kathryn snapped and attempted to burn the apartment. She was sent home. I had another eighteen months to stay because I was obligated to stay for three years because my family had joined me in Germany.

They say you can never go home again. If you ask me I will be quick to tell you that I did. As I look back it is as clear to me that it was God who directed my ship from the time I was conceived until this day. He still works in the lives of people to help them reach the unreachable, to comfort the weak and comfortless, and to be a light in a dark, dark world.

God was on my side, because I received a call from my old home town friend, Warrant Officer Leggs, who informed me that he and General Cunningham were retiring and encouraged me to apply for a direct appointment from an enlisted man to a Warrant Officer. I was approved by Congress, and was ordered to report to the U.S. Army Administration Center in Saint Louis, Missouri.

I could not believe the quick turn of events, one minute I was worried about our children and Kathryn's hospitalization, and the next minute I was headed home to try to make arrangements for someone to take care of my children. Although I was back in the states, I knew that when I was appointed to Warrant Officer I would have to go to Vietnam; as unpopular as the war was, it was still a war. As a soldier I was trained to take orders, and soon I would be giving orders to young men who could lose their lives in a war that no one understood; a war, that I predicted that no one would win.

As a soldier, white or black, you are isolated from the societal norms and belief processes of your country. We did what we were told, and like everybody else, most who thought that they were thinking for themselves, were only agreeing with the media; without questioning what they said, because after all, if it is in the paper it must be true. Besides the only paper that we received was the Stars and Stripes, a paper that was controlled by the four branches of service.

Put another way we had few if any reference points that would encourage dialogue. Even if there were the thought of disagreement with our leaders was looked upon as treason. We could not understand what all of the fuss was about as we read about the demonstrations in most major cities. We did not understand why Americans, good patriotic Americans, could demonstrate against their own country that was trying to protect them from communist aggregation.

As on schedule, I received a direct appointment to Warrant Officer with a specialty in Personnel and Finance. Kathryn was still in a mental institution but seemed to be on the road to recovery. It was during this visit that her mother died.

Having arranged for my mother to care for my children, I was assigned to an administration company the 527 Personnel Service Company that was being formed at Fort Lee, Virginia, it was there that I first heard about soon to be General Colin Powell.

One month later we were sent to Long Beach, California where we immediately embarked on a twenty day voyage to Vietnam; with a stop-over for two days in the Philippines to take on supplies. Shortly after our arrival, we were told that that the Viet Cong (V.C.) had started the "Tet Counter Offensive with the goal of toppling the Saigon Government.

All of the officers were briefed four days prior to our scheduled arrival date that Army Intelligence had reported that the (VC), had control of the city and the port of Qhi Nhon. We arrived at the port on January 3, 1968, and much to our delight, we were able to go ashore without firing a shot.

I served in Vietnam from January 1968 until the winter of 1970; With the exception of the six month hiatus at Fort Sheridan, Illinois, I came back to the same company each time.

During my second tour, I did almost as much work in my additional duty of Civil Action Officer, Race Relations Officer, and Sports and Recreation Officer as I did as Personnel Officer.

We made some significant inroads with the local people, many of whom became spies who helped in the arrest of a large number of Viet Cong soldiers.

When my first tour was over I was assigned to Fort Sheridan, Illinois. It was the Headquarters for the Fifth U. S. Army. When I reported for duty they really didn't know what to do with me because they knew that I was scheduled to return to Vietnam in six months.

They found a corner behind the receptionist counter, and instructed me to read the plans for the estate funeral for former president Harry S. Truman. My job was to update the master plan from change orders received from the Secret Service, the CIA, and the FBI. As usual I tackled my assignment with gusto, realizing that my supervisor was just trying to keep me busy. I noticed a page that outlined the procedure to be followed when the President passed away.

I noticed a reoccurring pattern that the Secret Service was concerned about. They were concerned that there wasn't enough lighting in the alley that led to the back entry of the mortuary in Independence, Missouri; it seemed that the person who owned and lived in the house that sat directly behind the funeral home for whatever reason refused to sell a piece of his land.

There had been several attempts, to no avail, to purchase a ten foot parcel of his front yard; in order to place a light pole on the corner of his property. There were several entries in the plans that summarized their attempts to buy the land but the owner refused to bulge.

When I asked my supervisor about the problem in question, he was surprised to learn that there was some concern on the part of the Secret Service, and casually mentioned that he was scheduled to make a summary, semi-annual visit, to fine tune the plans and seek any adjustments that Mr. Truman or the Secret Service desired.

As I was preparing to leave late Friday evening, my supervisor asked if I would like to drive down to Independence with him on Monday morning. I told him that I would be delighted to drive him there because although I lived in East Saint Louis, I had never been to Independence before, and hoped to get a glimpse of the President. He assured me that he would get approval from the Secret Service, and was sure that it could be arranged. Although I had a top secret security clearance in order to come within a hundred feet from the President, you had to give prior notice.

Sure enough we started early Monday and two hours later we were twenty five miles from Springfield, Illinois. An hour later we passed my home town, good old East Saint Louis. From my vantage point on the newly constructed U.S. Highway 70, I could see the old building that once was Saint Mary's High School.

Off in the distance I could see the Red Top Nightclub, long a fixture for the night life; especially on Sunday nights, because the bars closed in Saint Louis, Missouri a "lot of people" would come and hear the blues and Jazz greats; just name them, and you will find that they all played at one time or another, at the Red Top.

We stopped about twenty miles South of Saint Louis, Missouri, and had a light lunch; after which we proceeded to Independence; we arrived in the late afternoon. We checked into our rooms and retired early because the next day was to be pivotal for all of us.

I was not prepared for what happened when we arrived at 219 Delaware Street. There sitting in front of me was a pristine white two story house that had been in the Truman family for two generations. It had a total of fourteen rooms; with porches on each side of the main entrance. I later learned that there was an expansive porch that ran from one side of the house to the other.

As I was taking in this house that you only see in movies, The President came down the freshly painted wooden steps with ease. As he quickly pass our car, he asked as he looked straight at me, "who is he, and where did he come from." Momentarily I and my supervisor went numb, everything was moving so fast, it was the first the time in my life that I could not move.

Mr. Truman opened the passenger side himself and motioned me to get out of the car; he went on to say as he turned and said, let's be on our way, all of us seemed to move with one accord as if being directed by a drill sergeant. Boy could he walk!

I was even more astonished when he motioned for me to walk next to him. The secret service agent looked at me suspiciously as he reluctantly moved to give me space to walk. After about two minutes of silence, with my heart pumping from walking so fast, but mostly because I was actually in the presence of the man, who in fact had played a major role in the integration of the military.

He asked me many question about my life in the Army, where I had served, and how I was able to make the trip from Fort Sheridan. He went on to say how proud he was to have served in the Army as an Artillery Officer. I looked back at my boss, who shrugged his shoulders, and turned his palms to the sky, as if to say, you are on your own.

Somehow this calmed me, which gave me the nerve to look him straight in the eye, as I said, "Mr. President, I have come to help solve the problem about the light pole issue at the funeral home. He said a few words that I cannot repeat, and said, Good Luck!

After our walk and a cool drink of water, we set out to meet the man who refused to sale a small plot of his yard, no more than four feet by six; the colonel left me off at the front of the mortuary, under the pretense of checking on some detail with the owner. I learned on our joyous trip back to the fort, that he and the despiteful land owner had an argument about his lack of patriotism by not selling the government the required land.

As I approached I saw the owner trimming his hedges. I went straight up to him and said in my usual manner when talking to southern white men, "Howdy." He, like the president, said, "are you with them folks from up in Illinois? Again, I said, yes sur, using the southern dialect; he laid his sheers on the hedges and asked if I wanted some water. Although I had just had two full glasses at the "Truman House," I learned a long time ago that if you were trying to sell someone, something, get them to do something for you.

After I stretched my stomach to its limit after slowly drinking a tall glass of water, he said that I was the first colored soldier that he had seen come with what he called in a sarcastic way, that group. I knew that I would have to use every bit of persuasion and sales technique to pull off, this here to fore, impossible task.

It seemed that the problem was a long-standing personal issue with the land owner and the president; although he said that he voted for him, they were not on speaking terms. I inquired if he had been in the Army, and he began to tell me about the colored cook that helped him get through his three years during his stint in World War One. After listening patiently, as he paused to take a breath, I asked him if he would help me in memory of his benefactor in the Great War, it would surely keep me off the hot seat with my boss.

To my surprise, he said how much will they pay me, I told him that I thought the offer was five thousand dollars, he then said, "what the hell, ya'll can have it, but don't mess up my yard, I want it back the same way it was." I assured him that we would not tear up his yard.

I can't describe the feeling that was churning inside of me, as I told my boss about the events that had just occurred, at first he didn't believe me; it was not until I was granted the privilege of telling the President. I am sure that my boss thought to himself, that surely I would not lie to the President. I had the picture of me shaking hands with the land owner, with his name on the back, George something. It was lost in the fire in Germany.

I returned to Vietnam with renewed confidence. I again asked for and was given the worst additional duty of Civil Action Officer. Whose duty was to coordinate activities with the local village leaders, it gave me an outlet to help people who could not help themselves. There were many of the village leaders still there. There was one thing that we had in abundance of was food, and there was one thing I knew how to do was get food, which we distributed to people in the village town of Qui Nhon.

As Personnel Officer, I had the authority to reduce the tour in Vietnam by as much as fifteen days. I used this arbitrary authority to trade for food water, medical supplies, soccer balls, and yes cigarettes.

We gave mostly fruits and vegetables but during each Christmas we always made bags of candy, fruit, and gum. It was doing the Christmas of 1969 that I saw the callousness and indifference on the part of people who had almost nothing, in the trampling of a young boy as they jockeyed for a place to receive the food.

He died in my arms after we had untangled him from the barbed wire that seemed to encircle his whole body. That experience still haunts me to this day.

Because of my early encounter with high ranking Army Officers, and my subsequent chance meeting with President Truman, coupled with the fact that Warrant Officers were viewed with admiration from both officers and enlisted men; officers admired us for our technical ability, and our common sense approach to solving complex problems based on our vast knowledge of our specialty and our experience as Non Commissioned Officers.

Troops were being sent to Vietnam without their permanent records. They were being moved so fast during the first Tet Offensive, that they arrived in country with nothing more a shell of their official personnel record. The record that they brought with them, gave the name and address of the next of kin and the person designated to receive their death benefits.

By chance I walked into a building that was more than sixty feet long, and forty feet wide. When I inquired about the contents, my Sergeant told me that they were records of soldiers who we could not account for, and that we did not know whether they were living or dead.

After looking at no more than ten randomly selected records, I could not believe my eyes as I looked at the permanent record of Corporal Brodie Farrington, from Brooklyn, New York, by way of one of the Caribbean Islands. I quickly double checked to see where he was stationed in 1958, and sure enough we were in the same company at the same time during my tour in Korea in 1957 to 1958. As I casually looked through some of the orders in his record, I was shocked to see me and Bill Kunkel's name placing us on special duty to play baseball. Go Figure!

To say the least, the Army had "egg on its face." I suggested that we write a letter to the next of kin realizing that some of the men who these records belonged to might have lost their lives. At first I met with skepticism, but after I composed a letter, and after discussing the pros and cons my superiors approved the letter that we promptly sent out to every family.

The response was tremendous; some, including my comrade Brodie Farrington responded. He had retired and was living in New York City. He was happy to hear from me, and said the usual thing, "Whenever you are in New York give me a call."

We counted all of the records and found that there were one hundred and fifteen thousand records. We worked our usual seven days a week for six months and were able to locate over one hundred thousand families or soldiers who had served in Vietnam. I was given a "special efficiency report" which recommended that I be given a direct appointment to Captain.

The offer was tempting but I knew that when and if the war ended I would not revert back to my previous grade of Warrant Officer, but would return to my permanent grade of Sergeant First Class. Thank God, I knew "the rules of the road."

The enlisted men admired Warrant Officers because we all knew that at one time, we were one of them, and fought for them whenever the need arose. To put it bluntly, we didn't take any gruff from anybody, officer or enlisted. An example of this was during a visit by General William T. Westmorland, the commander of all troops in Vietnam. Our unit had solved a big administrative snafu by locating soldiers whose records were stored in our warehouse. I had a standing rule that you had to remove your hat unless you were "under arms" when you came into my office. To my knowledge the General had never been seen without his hat on.

On that fateful day everyone was chattering about what I would do if the General came in without a pistol. Sure enough he not only wanted to congratulate me but all of the troops who took part in accomplishing the task.

Our office was on the second floor and as soon as he walked in I calmly reached up and removed his cap and handed it to him, as I said, "I am sorry sir but my rule is the old army rule about wearing a hat inside while not under arms." He smiled and acted as if nothing had happened. My Colonel almost died for lack of oxygen. He thanked all of us and left almost as quickly as he had appeared.

As I reflect on my three tours, the only thing positive was meeting common ordinary people who had some of the same type of dreams for a better life for themselves and their children. I realized after my second tour, that we could not and would not win the war. We would simply pull out and leave the fate of the South Vietnamese in the hands of their oppressive neighbors to the North.

Although we did not win the military conquest, I felt that I had played a part in changing the lives of some of the people that I learned to a

When I returned to the states I had five years left for my long awaited retirement. I had heard about Atlanta mostly because it was the home of Dr. Martin Luther King, and about the Atlanta

University Complex. I was told a long time ago, about the wonderful opportunities for a black business man to prosper in Atlanta.

To my complete surprise I was given my first choice and was assigned to the 111th Military Intelligence Group as their Personnel Officer. My boss, who later became a good friend, Major H. W. Adams, gave me free reign to turn our personnel section into a top notch unit. The personnel unit had not passed their last annual inspection, and I was given forty five days to prepare for a re-inspection. I had a total of seven clerks, six women and one man.

The women were eager to learn, and had all of six months of actual experience in a personnel office. We quickly molded together, and through hard work and dedication beyond the normal duty hours, we passed the inspection with flying colors.

Two of the women were married and was having some difficulties, and sought my help. Through counseling and suggestions they were able to turn their marriage around.

It was doing this period that I coached my last basketball team. I had two big men. I called them the two D's Doyle, and Dahl. Dahl was from St. Louis and played for Oglethorpe in the Atlanta Area prior to being drafted. We beat everybody, we would come down the floor and dump the ball into the big men and watch them work. Both were great passers, it was like taking candy from a baby. It was quite fun.

Things were going good, but I was lonely. I noticed a young woman, Leola Faith Reed, who I thought was a civilian, but after checking I learned that she was a Warrant Officer in military intelligence.

I checked her file and learned that she was single. I am not sure how we met, but I remember taking her to lunch. She was smart

197

and somewhat shy, and aloof. I was attracted to her, and we began dating. In less than three months, we were married.

Faith, as she preferred to be called, lamented that the only thing missing in her life was a daughter. In my usual bravado I said "that's not a problem we can make it happen."

Since this was uncharted waters, I posed a hypothetical situation, and mailed it to the Special Actions Branch of the Adjutant General's Office I used Faith as an example; a woman, intending to make the Army her career, with a vast amount of experience, and clearly an asset to the military. Should she be allowed to remain in service, given light duty six months prior to term, and given six weeks of maternity leave, to bond with her child? In short, should she be allowed to remain in the Army? I received a call from the Adjutant General's Office in Washington, D.C.

The caller was a woman who asked me to make a formal request for a change in policy, before hanging up she said that it was a good chance that the policy might be changed. I told Faith and the women in my office what had happened and the news was met with enthusiasm. Four months later the rule was changed.

Although I knew that the regulation was being changed, I did not take any chances and before Faith got pregnant I requested an exception to the army policy, which would allow her to stay in service after having a child. At that time, a woman could volunteer for the service if she had school age children; but they had to leave the service if they got pregnant after joining, married or not.

Ten months later Evette Halcyon Cruise was born. We bought a house on Star Mist Drive less than three miles from Fort McPherson. We were happy, and we made friends in the neighborhood and settled into a normal life. Because Faith did not wear uniforms, she able to work until a week before our daughter was born.

All in all, things were great; I had a satellite office in San Juan Puerto Rico, and just had to visit them twice a year for a week of inspection and training. Playing golf there was crazy, one minute the sun was shining and the next, you could not see your hand in front of your face because of the downpour. And just as quickly as it started the rain would stop and the sun would return as if it had only taken a quick nap.

An order came from Washington directing that all officers be trained in race relations. Since I had the training and had acted in the capacity of a Race Relations Officer in Vietnam. I was given this thankless task to train all officers at Fort McPherson below the rank of General, the three Generals on post were trained at Forces Command Headquarters by a trainer from Washington, D.C.

I was given three days to prepare and the following Monday we began the training. Our first class consisted of nine white officers and one black officer. I was forced to call on all of my experience and my lack of fear of being with senior officers to pull this all off.

I taped the first session which lasted for three days, and was ready the following Monday for my second group. I had followed with both pride and some trepidation the career of my first cousin, Dr. Harry Edwards, who help mastermind the boycott of the Mexico Olympics. A (so called unpatriotic act) that occurred three years earlier, a demonstration that stuck in the crow of most people in the military.

First it was quite emotional; first of all, they didn't think that they needed any training, especially from a Black Warrant Officer. And secondly none of them viewed themselves as racist. Our one black Colonel told the class on the first day, with a statement that I had never heard before, and have only heard one time since.

"I don't see black I don't see white, I just see men! After this outburst you would have thought that you were in a Southern

Baptist Church in rural Mississippi, by the shouts of amen that he received at the conclusion of his speech.

Without fail, at the end of the fifteen week sessions, at least half of the men and women would say thank you. In fact one Colonel who was about to retire and return to North Carolina begged me to come and take over his human resources office at a large textile mill that his family had owned for over a hundred years.

Six months later I received a non retention letter from The Adjutant General's Office in Washington, D.C., giving me the option of being released from active duty or retiring with over fifty percent of my current pay.

What an easy choice I had to make. I immediately requested to be retired on May 1, 1974, exactly twenty years to the day, of my train ride to Fort Chaffee, Arkansas for basic training. Since my retirement was imminent, I was assigned to the Retirement Services Office. The position was being filled by a civilian who had done a good job by connecting retiring soldiers to jobs, often times before they actually retired.

He was retiring but had set up the first Retirement Services Retiree Council. A council composed of retirees who had served honorably and had retired through years of service or disability. Two members stood out in my mind, Command Sergeant Major Joseph Bussy and Max Cleland, a retired Army Captain who had to have both legs, and his right forearm amputated. I was amazed at his ability to take his wheel chair out of his car and the apparent ease of putting it back as he would leave our office. He later became a State Senator, as well as a U. S. Senator, and was later appointed to head the Veterans Administration by then President, Jimmie Carter. To my knowledge he still remains a loyal Democrat.

Sergeant Major Bussy in contrast to the public exposure that Senator Cleland received was instrumental in helping many retiring soldiers get good jobs with The Coca Cola Bottling Company.

He later helped me obtain some contractual work with his company. I will never forget the day that he gave me a personal tour of the company, and introduced me to Mr. Robert W. Woodruff, Chairman Emeritus of Coca Cola. He was a stately man and although he was declining in health, he was instrumental in helping me obtain a half million dollars cash grant to Morehouse College for their new medical school.

It is commonly believed and said by many, 'if you can't make it in Atlanta, you can't make it anywhere." I wanted to experience this saying, first hand.

After my retirement I opened a bar outside the rear gate of Fort McPherson, and took a job as Operations Officer for Norrell Security Company, a subsidiary of Norrell Personnel Services Inc. It was there that I had the pleasure of operating the first "Self Serve Gas Stations" in Atlanta, and maybe in the United States.

We used security guards without weapons, who were actually clerks, which enabled me to triple the number of women in our work force. It was during this period that I learned that the Devil does not care whether you do the wrong thing for the so called, right reason, or the right thing for the wrong reason.
At first, I truly believed that I was helping some of the needy women, while deep down, I knew that I was attracted to some of them.

In the end, I was not faithful to my wife, my company, or to my family. I spent more time helping others, many of whom, I did not get involved with, yet I was spending more time with them than I was with my family.

I felt that I was powerless to stop, I recalled the days when I was young, how I dreamed about having someone to love and admire me, just because of the me, that I really was, a man who wanted to share his love with others unconditionally.

I left Atlanta a broken man, ashamed of what I had caused to happen and I now realized that I needed to be with my family if I was ever going to get it right. I no longer felt that I exhibited the self assured, poised persona that I had perfected long ago.

I carried this burden until I met my wife Barbara, and thus began a healing process that eventually included God in my life. Oh how wretched I felt!

In my continued attempts to help the least fortunate, I made more money in Atlanta that I ever dreamed I could. But I was still spending most of it on people who I thought would become producers rather than takers, takers who honestly believed what they said, but was not ready to pay the price of success. Amid this turmoil I was in the process of cleaning up another mess that I caused, I was getting a divorce for the second time. It was the most difficult time of my life. I realized that you can do the right thing for the wrong reason, or the wrong thing for the right reason, both are wrong. I felt that I needed to be with my family, especially my mother. I left Atlanta with a set of golf clubs and two changes of clothing.

CHAPTER 23

BORN AGAIN

Here I was riding on a Grey Hound Bus through what is called The Grape Vine; a series of mountain peaks about one hundred and eight miles North of Los Angeles, California. It was from this vantage point that I first saw the city of Bakersfield, California.

After the driver successfully navigated up into the mountains with its never ending winding highway we were thrust from sea level up to over four thousand feet in less than fifty miles.

After reaching the summit at Fort Tejon Ranch we started the long stretch to the valley floor. As the driver drove through the last of the intermittent patches of fog and rain, I could clearly see the valley floor.

Here I was about to enter the city of Bakersfield, a place that I would soon call home. I had the strangest feeling that it would be here that I would find my reason for living and in a sense would find my new beginning and find inner peace.

It was early evening and the moon and the stars seem to jump into the heavens from behind the mountain peaks and the lights from the city beamed as little baby stars that miraculously survived their tumble from the heavens to the valley floor. Most cities look more beautiful at night than in daylight.

Bakersfield is an exception. It is beautiful under the scrutiny of daylight; with its grape orchids, citrus trees and ever present green lawns. It is a beautiful little town nestled at the base of the Sierra Nevada Mountains. Yet it is big enough to provide most of the things that the average person desires; the arts, recreation, churches, oh yes, many churches. Generally it still has the untapped potential to continue to be "An All American City."

I knew it was here that some way or somehow I would find my destiny. I came to California with a set of golf clubs, a small travel bag, and another puncture in my heart; wondering if it was all me or the trials that I had to go through before God could use me for His glory. As I recounted events in my life I wondered where I had gone wrong.

Here I was forty four years old, married twice and about to be divorced twice. I had left a wife who was a good woman, a woman that I admired, but I did not truly love her the way I wanted to love a woman. I wondered if I was the major problem and not her.

I concluded that I did not try hard enough and just gave up. I guess you could say that we did not share the same dreams, hers were built upon security, saving for the future and finally retiring to a quiet life in Atlanta. In contrast, I had dreams that included service to the community, taking risks in business and working for myself.

These dreams were cemented into my very being while I was yet a young boy and they continued to burn inside of me. In fairness to her, I did not give her a chance to understand and share those dreams.

As I looked back over my life, I concluded that as a young man, I was athletic, good natured, witty, and not to bad to look at. I had the gift to think on my feet, and take risks. With all of this going for me I was yet longing for something; something to fulfill my reason for being alive. These were the things that I mused over until suddenly the lights came on and the driver said in his bus driver voice Bakersfield.

As I continued to ponder, a feeling of relief came over me, and I heard a small voice, say "this is the place that you will find what you seek." My sister Wilma Freda Cruise-Ray, my mother and my oldest brother Floyd had moved to Bakersfield in part because our aunt Phedoshia-Wofford-Smith lived here.

She was part of the great migration from the southern states like Mississippi, Arkansas, Texas and Oklahoma. It seemed that everyone I met was born in Oklahoma or their parents were born there. They started migrating to California in the late 1930's, not in search for gold, but for a chance for a better life.

I rang Freda's door bell, and when she opened the door she had a look of disbelief in her eyes. We had not seen each other since 1968, just before my first tour of duty in Vietnam.

They were all quite surprised to see me standing there. After the usual hugs I told them that I was just visiting, and only intended to stay for the remainder of August 1978, and possibly the month of September.

I explained that I was in the process of getting a divorce and my intentions were to play some golf, see some of California, and return to Atlanta long before Thanksgiving.

I had no idea what God had planned for the rest of my life. My life like many others was a roller coaster with its thrills of success and failures because I was always trying to make a difference in the lives of others. My feelings of disgust during the low periods when I failed stirred me to fix the missing me, in me. I knew that I had to be patient and try to figure out how I could help myself before I tried to help anyone else.

My escape had always been sports. I was especially at ease on the golf course although it was a place where you were constantly reminded that you were black. Golf courses, the good ones that is, were the most prejudice places in the world on Sunday morning, only second to the church.

It was on the golf course that I found solace. Golfers are the zaniest, most fun loving trash talking group of people you will ever meet. In fact most of my Bakersfield group still play at an age when most men talk about the things they use to be able to do; they still show up at Sycamore Canyon Golf Course in Arvin, California between 8:30 to 9:30 every Monday morning.

Some of their pants sizes have changed in the waist, but yet, they still play. There are two groups, the long hitters, and as my barber, Mr. Key calls us, the scrubs. I decided on my seventy fifth birthday that I would return to golf, a game that I played as a young boy. My sister grew tired of my treks to the golf course and thought that I should apply for a position at the Annual Kern County Fair.

I was hired and assigned the job of taking tickets and greeting each patron. I greeted every one with the same enthusiasm as a Wall Mart Greeter. I was assigned another duty as parking attendant and I became a self appointed evaluator on the system used to conduct fair business.

On the last night of the fair I submitted an after action report to the consultant who was the director of admissions and parking. His day job was Director of Admissions at Knott's Berry Farm in Southern California.

A few days after the fair ended I received a call from him to tell me that he had read the report and he was going to recommend me to be the consultant for the following year. I was the first African American to obtain a contract to direct the admissions and parking. For, whatever reason September turned to October, and October to November. I realized that I could work three months out of the year, and by working three fair sites I could earn more than I earned working all year.

Because I was always on the golf course, my sister strongly suggested that I look for a job, or return to Atlanta. It wasn't because I was in need of money or security, I had enough of both. I too had grown tired of my care free life style, so I decided to take her advice and look for a job. I knew that I had to be patient and try to figure out how I could help myself before I tried to help anyone else. I interviewed for the job of Supervisor of Credit and Collection Department with Kern Medical Center.

The interview was short and to the point. My soon to be boss said that he would inform me by mail of their decision. As the interview was about to end, I boldly said, "If you don't hire me, you will be making a big mistake."

When I reached home he had left a message to call him; after the usual pleasantries he informed me that he had decided not to interview any more candidates and that he had decided to hire me. I was told to report to personnel office on Monday morning.

I continued to live with my sister and mother on 9th Street after returning from a trip to Mexico, we moved into a rental on Candleberry Lane. Our extended family was continuing to grow. In addition to my Aunt Phedoshia, there was Freda, her friend Thomas, my brother Floyd, and three of my five children Matthew, Carmen and Michael.

We lived directly across the street from Morgan Clayton an aspiring business man who had struck out on his own in the security business; today he is one of the most successful black business men in the county.

My sister would not take me serious when I gave her the same answer to her oft repeated question "What in the world are you going to do about a woman?" I had no idea that the answer was living less than ten minutes from our house.
In February 1979, my life took a turn for the better. I met my last wife, Barbara Jackson; she was engaged to a fellow at the time of our initial meeting.

I am sure that I was guided by my guardian angel to be at the most unlikely place to meet the woman who would help me start the healing process and through her love, her devotion, and her concern for me helped me find my reason to be me.

This is how I met Barbara Jackson! Freda had convinced me to go for a drink at the local Elks Club. At first I declined but she persisted and here we were, sitting in the only black bar in the area, not unlike most association type bars located in most cities in this country.

By comparison, it was a far cry from the Elks Club on the other side of town. It was run down and was built out of tin in a Quonset hut style. She began to ask the same question about me finding a woman, she said, "I know that you said that you are not interested in finding a woman, but to help me, what type of woman are you looking for?"

As I looked up I saw the waitress returning with my third round of Scotch. Out of the corner of my eye, I saw a woman entering the club; there was something about the way she walked, and the way she moved her arms, that first attracted me; as she got closer I could see that a man was walking close behind her.

My heart dropped and I was confused why I was feeling this way. I went back to doing small talk with Freda and suddenly I said, "The woman a few tables over from us, I would marry her." Freda turned her head like a swivel on automatic pitching machine and exclaimed, "Who are you talking about?"

I pointed to the woman in question; she was sitting as if she was the "Queen of Sheba just two tables over. I was dizzy, not from the drinks, and told Freda that the woman really interested me. When she saw who I was referring to, the "want to be" escort who followed her to her table talked to her for a few minutes before he went to the restroom. I asked Freda to go and ask her if the man seated with her was her husband. One thing that I was taught back in East Saint Louis was to be careful about talking to any woman if you are not sure if she isn't already "spoken for."

After what seemed like an eternity, and another three swigs of my drink, Freda returned and said "the man is not with her he was just trying to talk to her." When he returned I was in the chair that he had occupied. He paused at the table and proceeded to the bar and ordered a drink, all the while looking like a whipped dog.

The next thirty minutes were a blur. Barbara stopped me in my tracks almost before I could introduce myself. She went on to tell me that she was engaged and planned to be married; and the wedding was to take place soon after she graduated from the school of registered nursing.

She added that she was currently working as a Licensed Vocational Nurse. She went on to say, "I am flattered that you want to talk with me, but I only stopped to have a drink. I am headed to pick up my fiancé from work."

I was momentarily stumped, I knew that the next twenty or so minutes would have a great bearing on my future. I don't know why, I just knew. I have always said "I am the world's greatest salesman," and this was the time that I knew I had to be at the top of my game. I can't honestly remember what I said, but she did listen, and as I was about to do my sales close, time was running out, she said, "you look like a nice man, well dressed, and well spoken, but as I said, "I'm engaged."

After my third recovery from what was beginning to be a lost cause, I asked her if I could escort her to the car. Walking in front of her until we reached the door was like walking the plank of a ship.

I opened the door and motioned her to walk ahead of me, what a sight! As she was starting the car she rolled down the window and

I gave her my card and made some cavalier statement about not being able to call her, and I wished her future happiness, but in case things didn't work out, to please call me.

Two weeks later she called me about thirty minutes before completing her shift at Mercy Hospital. I knew who she was immediately. It seemed that she had some misgivings about her relationship, and for whatever reason, decided not to get married. I didn't care why I was happy to hear her voice.

We spent every available hour together, talking and sharing our dreams. Barbara had been married to her first husband Tommy Buchanan, and they had two children, Marla and Eric, and she had a son, Randy, by her first love.

I believed in my heart that I had finally gotten it right. Here was this beautiful woman who in some respects carried some of the same fears, but was so loving, so giving, and not appreciated.

I wanted to know about her. We enjoyed each other's company; we talked every night and day. She had an overstuffed chair to the left as you entered her apartment; it was as far as I went into her apartment except the day she cooked for me. I couldn't believe that I was in love with this beautiful woman, and she could cook.

Three months later on April 12th I asked her to marry me. On May 31, 1979, we were married; it was the day before she graduated from nursing school. After the official ceremony, we jumped the broom.

The next eight years were bitter sweet. Everything considered we had few problems with the two boys who were in high school when we got married. Many years earlier, Marla had gone to visit her father's sister in Erie, Pennsylvania. After repeated attempts by Barbara to get her back, she never returned. To this day we continue to try to establish a bond with her and her daughter, our grand children and great grand children.

My youngest son Michael had graduated from Bakersfield High School. Carmen had completed The School of Registered Nursing at Bakersfield College and started a storied career in nursing and hospital administration.

Several years later we became estranged even though we loved each other we remained in the same city. Carmen was diagnosed with terminal cancer in March 2010. I will forever be grateful to my brother Howard who took care of her until she died at the age of fifty on May 11, 2010. She was loved and respected by her Kern Medical Center co-workers and union members.

She was also involved in the organizing of the local union and became its President a few short months prior to her death. She fought tirelessly for worker rights. It was the most difficult time of my life. She did not want us to visit her or call. Like I said, it was difficult.

Our son Randy graduated from Bakersfield Junior College and continued his education at California State Fullerton, earning a degree in Criminal Justice. He then attended California State Dominguez Hill where he obtained a Masters Degree in Public Administration and finally a Masters in Educational Counseling from the University of Lavern.

He currently works as a Transitional Counselor for the County of Los Angeles helping young men to transition from the juvenile penal system back into the mainstream school system. Eric had the more natural gifts, although he did not receive top grades, he had a sharp mind. When the Rap sensation hit America he was one of the more gifted writers and entertainers in this new found industry. He won several contests against many of the young men who became stars in this new art form.

He was tragically killed by a police officer who shot him in the back on his twenty seconded birthday as he was running away from him. Barbara was notified by the coroner as she was making cookies for his birthday. We considered a lawsuit but decided that we could not fight city hall.

Although Barbara and I had discussed our need to start going to church soon after Eric was killed, it was not until a friend and associate died of a heart attack that we really began to seek a place that we could worship. As I said before I was a Baptist mostly because my mother was a Baptist.

I had an occasion to travel to Los Angeles California to speak at an awards banquet for a group of Southern California area car dealers. I was so busy traveling across the state conducting sales training, race relations and delivering motivational speeches from time to time. I hired a man to drive me across the state to the various functions because it was difficult to make connections to most California cities by air and because I could polish up my speech while traveling by car.

I met him at a sales training session about six months earlier. After we arrived in Los Angeles we had breakfast and he asked if we could attend church because we were not scheduled to arrive at the function for another four hours.

We attended a tent meeting on Figueroa Street where the late great preacher, Nokomis Yeldell from Nashville, Tennessee was preaching. For the first time in my life I learned that God had a specific plan to save mankind.

After some further teaching I was baptized into Christ on that very day for the forgiveness of all of my sins; it was August 3, 1983. It took me several years to accept the fact that God had forgiven me of all of the sins that I had ever committed. I carried the weight of guilt long after God had relieved me of my burden through the blood of Jesus Christ. I have tried to be a faithful fruit bearing Christian since that day.

For the next ten years I sold everything from hair products, soap, to telephone service. Much of my success was due to the help of a young man from Jamaica by the name of Lawrence Watson. We founded a Gas and Electric Procurement Group, called The California Gas Procurement Group, Inc., (CGPG, Inc.).

We founded the company in anticipation of the soon to be deregulation of the utility industry in the State of California. All parties who desired to participate were required to attend briefings held by the utility companies. We learned that the utility companies were in fact, glorified transportation and maintenance companies. We immediately noted that we were the only black attendees, and the only non industry people in attendance.

Lawrence was learning the technical side and I was learning the language. To do anything of substance, you have to know both. We worked as one and made contacts with other companies who were capable of obtaining the gas and electricity but they had no idea of how to acquire customers. Our dilemma was just the opposite. In hind sight we should have become a marketing arm of one of those companies. We made the mistake of trying to do things that we were not capable of doing.

We trained over five thousand associates to go door to door to acquire small customers, which we bundled into a large customer base. In California it was called deregulation, and in less than six months we had acquired the agency rights to purchase gas and electricity for over a half million metered customers.

We did meet with a few companies but felt that we could purchase our own gas. We were led to believe by the bank that if we could prove that we had actual customers, it was almost a formality that we could get a three hundred million dollar line of credit from a large Northern California Bank who was having difficulty finding suitable minority businesses to lend money to. We were promised the same type of loan that the utility companies obtained based on the historical use of our customers.

After we produced the evidence that we had a large customer base who had given us the authority to act as their agent to purchase their power needs, the rug was pulled out from under us.

I was called to a meeting at one of the local law firms that represented one of the largest utility companies in Kern County. I was informed that the line of credit was not forthcoming. Again we were so close to helping hundreds of people to escape poverty.

The word spread fast, and we were courted by the major gas suppliers and marketers in Dallas and Houston, Texas. Things were still moving fast, we had amassed over a half million customer meters from all over the state, a feat that was accomplished in eight months. Because we had captured such a large part of the market, but never sold them any gas, I believe that the giants of the industry convinced the California Utility Commission that deregulation would not work in California.

In my continuing efforts to help people in poverty I started a lot of different businesses. All of which showed some promise, and created some hope. As I look back, we should have focused on the core business of marketing gas and electricity.

An example of our involvement in other unrelated businesses, our company purchased The Bakersfield Jammers, a local "D" League Professional Basketball Team. We bought the team out of Bankruptcy Court. Our purchase was contingent upon our approval by the league.

There was great local support and some people wanted to invest in the team. We were never approved by the league in part because we were labeled as "drug dealers," because we literally came out of nowhere, and "The only way they could afford the lifestyle that were living, they had to be selling drugs."

I wrongfully blamed the league president, Mr. Terdema Ussery, II a black man born and raised in Watts; how could he stand by when the league made a decision to deny us a license. I was so naïve. I thought if you were the commissioner you could say yes, when others were saying no. Not getting the license to operate was a blessing from God. We would have lost our shirts.

We re-directed our attention to helping more than ten or twelve men running up and down a basketball court. We continued to hire men and women to work in our landscaping business a feat made possible by the President of Castle and Cooke, Glen Hierlmeier. With the help of this influential angel we was able to assist many people in the low income community change their standard of living. We developed a plan for the company to hire forty men and women to perform landscaping work for his company.

He received approval to advance a loan of one hundred thousand dollars with the stipulation that it would be repaid from our future earnings. I believe that it was his commitment to this task of redistributing wealth that cost him his job. Although we don't see each other very much he remains a dear friend.

As it is with most of us who dare to dream and desire to better the lives of others (a high risk calling at best), Barbara and I continued to probe to find ways to help others. We formed a masonry and cement construction business in 2004, we hired over seventy five men, mostly Mexicans because there were less than five young blacks qualified to do quality work.

We were able to build a relationship with several builders and land developers. Phil Gaskill, of Gaskill Custom Homes was very helpful in our landscaping and concrete business.

215

With glowing references from Castle and Cook, we began to land some large jobs mainly in landscaping. We continued to make a profit until the down turn hit the construction and housing industry. After holding on for several years, we closed the business in December 2007.

CHAPTER 24

THE LONG WAY BACK HOME

I contracted Valley Fever in 2008. It is a disease found mostly in a few Western States. It attacks the lungs. It is a disease that has flu like symptoms which sometimes make it hard to diagnose. In severe cases gone untreated the disease can be fatal. It was during my fight to regain my health that I was introduced to Micro Financing. It is a business popularized by Dr. Muhammad Yanus an economist and founder of the Grameen Bank in Bangladesh.

As I lay in bed watching television one early morning in April 2009, Dr. Yanus explained how anyone could help people who desired to better their economic circumstances. He said that the Grameen Bank made loans to women in third world countries. The bank's customer base is over ninety percent female, most of whom live in third world countries.

It was the first time that I heard the term micro financing. It is a system founded and popularized by Dr. Yanus who was explaining how he started in 1976 by lending a small group of women in Bangladesh enough money to start a small business. He added that he believed that western women were not good candidates for this type of business because they do not have the background of extreme poverty nor the temperament to stay the course.

Although I was sick I was convinced that I could do the very same thing. I contacted the main bank in Bangladesh and was directed to their web site. In less than a week I had a general understanding of how the system worked.

As I pondered on how I could best make this happen I recalled that my church and other congregations outside Bakersfield had sent money to Kenya for the purchase of Bibles for Christians in Uganda.

Although I was still recovering from my illness I was driven and sure that this is what God wanted me to do. I forgot about my health and against my wife's advice as well our friend Jill Trice, a medical doctor who lives in Southern California I continued to make plans to start the project.

After many emails, telephone calls, and prayers, my wife and I set up a parent corporation in Nevada, and a subsidiary corporation in Bumala, Kenya. Through faith we were able to attract the following people to help us in this great work. Without these people this project would not have happened.

The Cypress Church of Christ
Bill Carter from the Cypress, California Church of Christ
Jesse and Jill Trice from the Cypress Church of Christ
Steve Garner a good friend and local business man
Marcie Davis from Houston, Texas
Wilma Davis, California Avenue Church of Christ
Ysidro Porter, California Avenue Church of Christ
James, Jr. and Sheri Hosey, California Avenue Church of Christ
Blas Gonzales a good friend from Bakersfield, California
Renard Vine a good friend from Pasadena, California
Gambino Esquivias, our landscape/gardener
Glenn Jones and the brethren at the Church of Christ in Kiel, West Germany

We began by training two staff people using the Grameen Banking Model. We funded the first five women on May 11, 2009. The response was unbelievable! In less than a month we had funded eighty women and one man whose name was Matthew Opono.

After four months at the request of the staff in Kenya and the directors from our parent company I planned a trip to Kenya for early February, 2010. I told my wife that I would not go if my doctor advised against it. My specialist Dr. Augustine Munoz, and my primary physician and the other fine physicians and staff at

The Kern Faculty Medical Group saw the desire in my eyes, and my determination to go, said, "go but you can't stay any more than three weeks, and you must continue to take your medicine while there."

As a result of the tremendous response by our investors and the success that we experienced we were able to fund over one thousand women in a seven month period. All of whom are repaying their loans ahead of schedule.

Word spread like a prairie fire in Kenya. In addition to the women that we loaned money to we registered over ten thousand women for future funding.

Alfred Kaisiano a local minister at the Church of Christ in the city of Bumala was hired to supervise the lending effort. Bumala is a town in Western Kenya located less than thirty kilometers from the Ugandan Border.

Over fifty thousand people come to the open market in Bumala every weekend. Many of whom had heard about the micro lending that was being offered in Bumala.

Alfred was so overwhelmed with church work because the membership swelled from fifty to over one thousand in the seven months even though the women were told that they did not have to come to church in order to get a loan. But because of the growing number of new borrowers he hired Dorothy Acheing a church member who had experience working in micro financing while living in Nairobi.

Alfred died unexpectedly from exhaustion and malaria. It was such a shock to me personally and professionally. Alfred called me "Mzee" which means old man in Swahili. His death was a great loss to us all. After Alfred's death the day to day operations were entrusted to Dorothy. Fred Ongara returned to Kenya from Belfast

Northern Ireland. He returned home to replace Alfred as the Minister of the local church.

Dorothy and Fred lied from the beginning. They had been married for several years but Dorothy told me Fred was married to her sister who was a lawyer living in Northern Ireland.

When I arrived in Kenya Dorothy had three children, the youngest of whom she named Freddie Cruise. I asked her if I had ever told her my father's name because that was the name of my father. She said "the name just came to me."

Dorothy and Fred had a son named Carl. He had been badly burned on the back of his head and neck. Through the help of a church in America he received treatment for his injuries in San Antonio, Texas. After my return from Kenya in February 2010, I received a picture from a church located in Turkey where Fred and Dorothy lived some years earlier as husband and wife along with all of their children, including Carl.

At first the business continued to grow but the financial reports were at best sketchy. We sensed that something was wrong and the share holders gave me permission to go to the land that I had so long dreamed about visiting.

I could not believe that I was on my way to the very place that I had so long desired to see. As I boarded the plane in Los Angeles I thought about my brother James.

At last I was headed to Kenya by way of England and Saudi Arabia. Twenty eight hours and three seat companions later I arrived in Nairobi.

Like President Obama when he traveled to Kenya, my bags were left in Saudi Arabia and would not arrive in Nairobi until Friday, which delayed my trip by car to Bumala for two days.

Little did I realize that the real problem was waiting for me at the airport in the person of Fred Ongara. He was holding a sign with my name written in large red letters. He had the widest smile I had ever seen. He claimed to have just arrived from Belfast, Northern Ireland a few days earlier.

Fred's father had been a hard working minister to rural villagers of Western Kenya for over thirty years. Fred followed in his father's footsteps but his motive was not to save souls but to feed his greed through his lies and fraud.

Believing that I was working with honest Christian people I failed to see the obvious signs. Our computer which stored all of the financial information for Pull Up From Poverty, Inc, Kenya had been mysteriously broken.

I was told that the computer could not be fixed. When I inquired about retrieving the data from the hard drive they assured me that they could do it but it would take three days. A week later when I inquired about the financial information Fred said that the computer was in the shop and would be fixed in a few days, but I never saw it again.

I was also told that the house where we lived while waiting for my bags was located in one of the nicest areas in Nairobi. Fred said that the house belonged to his friend who was an engineer working in Germany. Fred claimed that he was going to call and introduce him to me but he never did. I now believe that the house belonged to Fred and Dorothy.

Friday finally came and sure enough my baggage was waiting at the lost and found. The next day we began our journey to Bumala. The trip took ten hours because the road was barely passable by car. It was the most tiring trip that I ever taken. There were four people in the back and three in the front of a mid-sized Honda.

Fred's son Carl, who had first and second degree burns from the top of his head to the base of his neck had to sit between my legs on the edge of the front passenger seat. He sat between my straddled and aching legs for the entire trip. As I said I can't recall a trip as physically demanding as the one to Bumala.

My plan was to stay at least one night in a village but after seeing the grass hut with its dirt floor and the bed that I was to sleep on I realized that I had to move to the Border Palace Hotel. It was clean but somewhat primitive. The food was average and the cook had no idea what a scrambled egg was. After two failures I finally convinced him to allow me to show him how to soft scramble eggs. He started asking other customers if they wanted their eggs scrambled. We left early in the morning to meet some of the ladies.

As I walked through the market place on my first weekend I was overwhelmed by the show of love for our works there. I was amazed at the variety of goods being sold. There were women who made ropes used to steer cows and other small animals. At first glance I thought to myself, "How can they make money selling rope?"

It was not until the animal auction ended that I realized the need for rope. Most people who purchased cows, purchased a rope to walk their animal home otherwise the animal may be killed if it suddenly bolted into heavy traffic moving in both directions at a high rate of speed.

Prior to my trip to Kenya we purchased several buildings which included a former Teacher's College in the Busia District located between Uganda and Bumala. We purchased the buildings to house one hundred and sixty eight orphans who we transported from the City of Rongai located about thirty five miles from Nairobi. I was directed by our board to determine the status of the property in addition to checking on the progress of our micro finance business.

We were concerned because we never received the deed although the transfer of the property was handled by an attorney.

The first place we went after I checked into the Border Palace Hotel was the Teachers College. It was being renovated into a hotel and it was nothing like the pictures sent to us before the so called purchase took place.

Instead of the nice red brick buildings shown in the pictures that were sent to us the buildings were made from adobe and painted white. The former owner sold the property twice and on the night that he left Kenya for India he assured Alfred that the deed was forthcoming.

Fred claimed that the judge had awarded us some land owned by the first buyer to help recoup some of our money. To date we have not received the title to that land. I recently learned that Fred is running from the law because he owed a large hotel bill at the Border Palace Hotel. He told the manager that I was going to pay the bill. The manager called to inform me that Fred was in jail.

The crowning blow was when I received a fake death certificate indicating Dorothy had died. I have since learned that she and Fred are alive and well living in Kenya or Uganda.

It is now obvious that Fred Ongara is a con man who has received money from Christians all over the world; that he was married to Dorothy and he has used many different names in his diabolical schemes as a Minister/Evangelist.

In spite of the many setbacks that we have experienced we were fortunate to hire Erick Otieno Ongech, a young Kenyan who continues to do this most rewarding work. He registered our Corporation with the District Administrators and has started making loans to women in Sega, a city located between Bumala and Kisumu. With the help of his family he has organized a Non

Governmental Organization (NGO) that will be eligible for funds from the United Nations within the next five years.

I remained in Kenya for a total of twenty one days to encourage the women and the local leaders. Their show of love for this work and for the people who are assisting in this undertaking cannot be explained with words-you'd have to see for yourself. The country is unbelievably beautiful as the more than eight hundred pictures that we took during my visit will attest.

Kenya is a country where daily survival is the order of the day. The people and especially the women work from the time that the sun rises until after it goes down. On the other hand many of the men have totally given up hope and go to the same spot near the road and drink until evening. When they return home they seldom have a kind word to say to their wives. Most of the women have a deep desire to educate their children. It is the most sought after dream by every parent. It was a topic that always came up when I visited the women; they wanted their children to get an education.

In fact, one man a Mr. Michael Ognech traveled from Sega by bus seeking assistance to help bring his son Erick to America. He wanted his son to attend South Western Christian College located in Terrell, Texas. Erick has applied and will be accepted into the class of 2012-2013.

As fate would have it, God choose this same Erick a 23 year old young man to direct our current micro lending efforts. Sadly, he was chosen after the crooks Fred and Dorothy had stolen more than one hundred thousand American dollars; monies earned through micro financing and other monies sent to help take care of the widows and orphans.

I am often asked why I did not detect a problem while I was there. There are several answers, one I could not speak Swahili, and secondly Fred and Dorothy were professionals at stealing money from well meaning people.

Not to dwell on what has happened the cover was removed and the fraudulent plot was discovered. Most of our investors were discouraged and have stopped sending money to continue this great work. However, Barbara and I and our brethren in Kiel, West Germany continue to sacrifice and send money each month to continue our micro financing there.

Erick Ognech has taken on the task of lending money to women who have demonstrated leadership qualities and integrity. He is also raising the standards of this great effort to empower women in Kenya. After starting all over again we have funded over three thousand women who are paying back their loans at record pace.

Our goal was to fund twenty thousand women before the second anniversary of our corporation, Pull Up From Poverty (PUFP) inception. We strongly believe that we will reach our goal.

Kenya is a nation that is tribal by tradition, which can present many problems for the average Kenyan. The elite have the political power and are in control of money distribution. Unlike the financial system of the "have and have nots" micro financing is solving the problem of the third world poor. We have so many applicants we had to use a lottery selection system until we obtain more capital.

During the last week of my visit I had a strong desire to visit Mama Sarah Husein Obama, the paternal step grandmother of President Obama. The first time I heard her name was during the swearing in of President Obama. I had no idea that I would soon meet this strong passionate woman.

I read the President's book 'Dreams of My Father' during my flight to Kenya. When I mentioned her name to the people who met me at the airport it was apparent that Mama Sarah Obama was a legend in Kenya.

Although the trip to her compound was no more than twenty miles from what is liberally called a highway due to the almost impassable dirt roads and gigantic seemly endless holes, it took us over two hours to finally arrive in Kogelo, Kenya the home of Mama Sarah. I noticed that a school located just around the corner had been named after then Senator Barach Obama.

After going through a police sign-in we were given an introduction by a young lady who seemed to appear out of nowhere. After she completed a short briefing we waited about ten minute until a woman who walked as though she was in control came from her house. Her pace was brisk and her walk decried her age and with a high pitched voice she said, "Welcome."

There was a group of about eight Kenyan Students and their Professor who was ahead of us who mostly wanted to take pictures with her. They asked a few question and unlike many similar situations I encountered around the world there was no cost for taking pictures.

After they left she turned her attention to my group which included Dorothy, her four children and Fred Ongara, and Marion who I was told was a friend that Dorothy attended school with but I later learned was Fred's other wife. All three of them were participating in lies, deceit, and fraud.

Mama Sarah asked through an interpreter, "Who is the American?" I suppose the woman who gave us our orientation had reported to Mama Sarah that there was a black American waiting.

I noticed as she was talking with the students she appeared to be distracted as she continued talking with the adoring students. As I walked forward she motioned me to sit next to her while at the same time shouting over her shoulder, "Acheing, Acheing, Acheing.

I heard the screen door slam shut and saw a young man who looked to be no more than 25 years old running in our direction. It was Nelson Acheing, Mama Sarah's personal assistant. He could speak English very well. He told me that his name in Swahili meant I was born at noon.

He had a pad in his hand that had an imprint of a girl's foot. I later learned in a private conversation with him that they were trying to get the shoe sizes for the one hundred girls that Mama Sarah was helping; girls who were also orphans from the post election violence of 2007.

As I looked into the face of this strong woman I imagined that she must have been over eighty years old but she looked a lot younger than her age. She looked directly into my eyes but addressed her words to Nelson who was translating and said, "Really, a black man, from America? What are you doing here? I don't recall a black man coming here since my grandson visited us before he became president."

She wanted to know if my ancestors were from Africa. I told her that my family did in fact come from Africa and was sold to slave traders in Zanzibar. She laughed and said that is where her husband had been a slave before he returned to his tribe after working in Nairobi for some time.

She asked about our work in Kenya and who was sponsoring the effort? When I informed her that it was some ordinary citizens she was shocked. I had to repeat it two or three more times and when I looked at Nelson he said, "She understands what you are saying but it is hard for her to believe it."

We continued for another two hours talking mostly about helping girls to get an education and helping women to start a business. She showed a keen interest in what we were doing in Bumala.

To my surprise she told Nelson to give me her business card which I still have with her checking account number stamped on the back. She also mentioned that she would be willing to form an association with PUFP Kenya to help women and girls in her area.

I told her that I wanted to send some clothing and shoes to her but I feared the cargo might not arrive without some difficulty. She assured me nothing would happen if I addressed the cargo to her foundation. I have since learned that her foundation is losing items sent to her for the children.

She seemed to tire and I suggested to Nelson that we continue to exchange information and that Mama Sarah could return to her house. Nelson agreed and she stood up and said, "Good bye." As she started toward her house she asked if I was coming back to Kenya. I promised her that I would return in February 2013. She turned back, shook my hand and said for the third or fourth time, "Good man." I promised Nelson that I would also gather support for their foundation before I returned to Kenya.

I noticed the compound for the first time. I looked around and noted that her house had a tin roof, with a T.V. Satellite Dish and an evaporative cooler. It also had a generator. To the left front of the house there were two graves, one of the President's father, and the other of his grandfather. I was given permission to take pictures of both graves.

There were several chickens and one turkey in the yard; it appeared that the Turkey did not want any company. He kept spreading his wings in what appeared to be a threatening manner. I was glad when he decided to find a spot to rest in the shade.

We returned to Bumala with the exciting news that we had met Mama Sarah Obama. However, very few believed us until we showed them the pictures that we had taken with her, (Page 113).

One month after my return home I had a slight relapse with Valley Fever, and did not touch this book until I met Otis L. Cavers from Cleveland, Ohio, a rabid, die hard football fan of "The Ohio State University." We hit it off right away, and upon learning that he had some writing experience decided that we would help me finish the last two chapters of the book. Part of the proceeds will go to assist in financing our efforts in Kenya.

You may ask why Kenya and to be honest I don't know. I just knew that it was where the Lord wanted me to start. As I have stated before my dream is to help women in America to pull up from poverty.

But due to the many regulatory issues and hoops that one must jump through, not to mention the amount of money required to organize a lending institution, it seemed that the answer is to start in a third world county where a loan of two hundred dollars would enable a woman to start her own business.

Although Dr. Yanus was of the opinion that micro financing would not work in America, Grameen America was started in New York City, and the interesting thing that I have noticed most of the initial borrowers are from the Dominican Republic. Most of their initial funds came from corporate partnerships but Grameen America is now soliciting donations from ordinary citizens to help its efforts to grow.

As I look ahead I see the answer to not only solving the problems of poverty in the third world but through earnings from our third world efforts we will help eliminate poverty in the ghettos of America. Like everything else it is a numbers game.

The effort to help women to improve their life in Africa is the continuing legacy of the Cruise family and personally the greatest opportunity for me to serve mankind. This is the greatest honor that I have the pleasure of being involved in.

I thank all who have encouraged me and those who have supported this great work. Mostly I thank my wife who although she did not understand what drove me she stood by me through the good and the bad times.

And again to my brother James, and my grandfather James both of whom, still live in me. I thank God for molding me into the servant that I hope that I am becoming.

Finally I want to thank the mother of Charlie Cruise, a woman born in Africa, and all of her descendants who dreamed that we would be givers to our society.

Our story has not ended in fact it is just beginning. Look for our next novel "Redistribution of Wealth In America, scheduled for release in April 2013. We may change the title to "The Black Book." Stay tuned.

ABOUT THE AUTHOR

MATTHEW CRUISE

This story gives a documented vivid account of the struggle that the Cruise family had to endure in rural Mississippi. It started in the Blue Ridge Mountain of Picken County, Georgia, and takes us through the most difficult period of enslavement. It also tells about the murder and intimidation of the descendants of ex-slaves; the story continues with the decision to move to Illinois. The story stops, but does not end, with the return by Matthew Cruise, a descendant of Charlie Cruise to Kenya, to their original homeland. Even though this story is about the Cruise family, it is a story that we can all relate to.

Matthew is a compassionate activist who has devoted the last thirty five years as a mentor, a business man and with his wife Barbara have embraced the Christian faith. "We started to help women in Kenya to better their lives and by the grace of God we have affected the lives of over two thousand women. As I look back at my life I can't put a finger on the date that I decided to try to help the poor. I suppose it started when I lived in poverty with a family of ten.

17120186R00123

Made in the USA
Charleston, SC
27 January 2013